THE EARLY YEARS

The Open University Press
Children with Special Needs Series

Editors

PHILLIP WILLIAMS
Professor and Head of the School of Education,
University College of North Wales, Bangor.

PETER YOUNG
Formerly Tutor in the education of children with
learning difficulties, Cambridge Institute of Education;
educational writer, researcher and consultant.

Both Phillip Williams and Peter Young were members
of the Warnock Committee of Enquiry into the Education
of Handicapped Children and Young People.

This is a series of short and authoritative introductions for parents, teachers, professionals and anyone concerned with children with special needs. The series will cover the range of physical, sensory, mental, emotional and behavioural difficulties, and the changing needs from infancy to adult life in the family, at school and in society. The authors have been selected for their wide experience and close professional involvement in their particular fields. All have written penetrating and practical books readily accessible to non-specialists.

Children with Special Needs

THE EARLY YEARS

Maurice Chazan and Alice F. Laing

THE OPEN UNIVERSITY PRESS
Milton Keynes

The Open University Press
A division of
Open University Educational Enterprises Limited
12 Cofferidge Close
Stony Stratford
Milton Keynes MK11 1BY, England

First published 1982

British Library Cataloguing in Publication Data
Chazan, Maurice
    The early years.—(Children with special
    needs).
    1. Handicapped children
    I. Title II. Laing, Alice III. Series
    155.4'51   BF723.E9

    ISBN 0-335-10050-3
    ISBN 0-335-10052-X Pbk

Typeset by
R. James Hall Typesetting and Book Production Services
and printed by Anchor Press Ltd, Tiptree.

CONTENTS

EDITORIAL INTRODUCTION

The course of children's development is heavily influenced by the experiences of the early years. Indeed, many authorities attach as much significance to the four or five years before the start of formal schooling as to the whole of the rest of childhood and adolescence. It is in these first few years, for example, that language emerges and grows explosively, that the ability to make good human relationships is displayed and that mobility, the key to so many advances, is achieved.

For children with special needs, skills such as these are desperately important, and the need to acquire them effectively and early has been widely recognized. For example, education for children with impaired hearing has long been provided years before the start of compulsory school attendance. The Warnock Report on the Education of Handicapped Children and Young People accepted this view of the significance of the early years and urged that the extension of education for the under fives should be one of three priorities for action. What was acknowledged to be good practice has become a priority policy.

These considerations would alone be sufficient justification for including a book on the early years in this series on children with special needs. But there is another equally powerful argument. The series is directed at parents as well as teachers. "Parents as partners" is an important slogan which stands for a widely-supported approach to special education. Nowhere is this partnership more obvious and more essential than in the education of very young children, where parents are the first teacher and the home the first classroom.

The authors of this book, Maurice Chazan and Alice Laing, have written widely on many topics concerned with the education of children with special needs, but recently their work has centred on the key questions of these influential early years. On behalf of the Warnock Committee they undertook a critical survey of the needs of families of young handicapped children and the first two chapters of this book draw attention to some of the difficulties that parents face in securing adequate support at this time and to some of the schemes and programmes that have been introduced to help.

The central chapters discuss the kinds of educational experience that young handicapped children require. Snapshot descriptions of five children, each with his or her own special needs, illustrate the importance of presenting a separate programme for each child. Here again, these chapters stress the value of collaboration and partnership between home and school so that the traditional gap between the two is bridged.

The final section of the book focuses on children's language and behaviour problems. These are two areas of particular concern to parents and teachers and are the two areas with the highest proportion of problems in this age group. The appendices offer key suggestions for further reading and for useful materials and resources.

The book is soundly based on research findings, yet written in a clear and non-technical manner. For teachers of pre-school children, for those who work in any capacity with young children with special needs, and for parents, this survey covers some of the central issues of concern to them. But the early years are also the foundation years and for this reason everyone involved in special education will find something of interest and value in this contribution.

Phillip Williams
Peter Young

1

SPECIAL NEEDS
IN THE EARLY YEARS

In recent years, interest has increasingly come to be focused on the educational needs of young children prior to their entry into formal schooling. Children with special needs are no exception to this trend. The Warnock Report[1] for example, in reviewing the whole area of special educational treatment, considered the provision of education in the early years to be one of its three main recommendations. The reason for this interest lies in the importance of the early years for future development. Any loss of experience which may result from a handicapping condition is compounded as children grow older. While it may be possible to make good at a later date some of the adverse features of handicap in the early years, very often patterns of behaviour and expectation, established in the young child, persist.

HANDICAP IN YOUNG CHILDREN

Opinion today is, probably quite rightly, against the use of the label "handicapped". As a term it is often unacceptable to parents and not particularly useful to the professionals involved with the child concerned. Parents feel that the term indicates a permanent stigma, a barrier in the way of 'normalization' or integration with the non-handicapped, and professionals are not helped towards planning a programme by merely accepting a label. For handicap is not always a permanent condition. A child may be handicapped at one time of life and not at another. For example, even mild mental handicap may prevent a pupil from being successful in the classroom but may not affect out-of-school or post-school adjustment. Likewise, in young children, some developmental "landmarks" may occur as normal although others may be seriously delayed or even non-achievable. Failure to realize the selective nature of many handicaps may lead to a more extensive lack of development than need have been. For teachers, it is only too easy to accept the label "handicap" as meaning a difference, or even a deficit, in the child which will prevent progress, and so fail to discover ways of circumventing the problem.

The suggestion of using the term "special needs" rather than "handicap" is, therefore, an acceptable one. It implies that, with special help, children in such a category can achieve progress, although the extent of that progress will be determined by the nature of the problems affecting each individual. It implies also that consideration of the content and the location of the education to be offered to a child with special needs must be undertaken on an individual basis rather than on the basis of any special category, as each child has different special needs.

It is not always easy to identify special needs in young children and this is particularly the case with the very young. Identification is inevitably based on comparative judgements, that is, on the extent to which the child's development in any area is not in keeping with what would be expected. A child who is not talking at twelve months may present no problem, but if the child is still not talking at thirty-six months, a different judgement might be made. There is, therefore, a tendency for the number of children thought to be in difficulties to increase over the years, especially once the children are faced with school-type tasks. A similar increase is seen at adolescence but thereafter the numbers tend to drop, as many with special needs in school find themselves able to make an adequate adjustment in the community.

PREVALENCE OF SPECIAL NEEDS

Identification of special needs is largely dependent on situations in which certain aptitudes or abilities are called for and are not available. It is, therefore, difficult to provide exact percentages of the prevalence of such needs. It is also the case that a number of minor difficulties may obstruct a child's development as effectively as a major problem in one area. Again, what is seen as being 'a handicap' in one family may be tolerated with ease in another. Diagnosis, therefore, may not be a matter of any great precision, except in cases of severe and permanent handicap.

With regard to mental handicap, there would appear to be a measure of agreement on a rate of just over 3 per 1000 being severely retarded in the 5—11 age group. Behavioural deviance is much more difficult to estimate as the figure reached varies with the rater and the locality in which the rating takes place, as indeed do other estimates of handicap, including mild or moderate mental handicap. Figures ranging from just over 10% to just over 25% have been found for behavioural disturbance. It must be remembered, however, that there is considerable overlap between the various handicaps, so that a child who is intellectually retarded, for example, may well also have problems in physical or emotional development. Mild or moderate difficulties are not easy to estimate in any aspect of development. The Warnock Report[1] offers as an overall guide the figure of one in five children who 'at some time during their school career will require some form of special educational provision' (p.41).

A recent research survey carried out by the authors[2] would lend support to the estimated rate of prevalence suggested above. This study showed that in the selected sample, which consisted of all the 4-year-old children born in a certain six months in 1972 in two fairly large counties, 21.4% were judged to have special needs of a mild, moderate or severe nature which required further investigation. Eighty-three per cent of the children with special needs had problems in more than one area of their development and, as is usually found, more boys than girls were identified as having developmental difficulties. The highest proportion of problems was found to be in either speech and language development or emotional and behavioural adjustment.

Speech and language development are of particular importance in young children and will be discussed in Chapter 5. Not only does language enable children to understand their environment with precision, it is also an efficient vehicle for memory and for establishing social relationships. Poor or retarded linguistic development is particularly detrimental to the child's progress in any formal setting, such as the nursery class or the playgroup. It is, therefore, important that health visitors and others involved in the care of the young child should be alert to, and able to advise on, any difficulties in this area. With regard to behavioural problems, the authors' study showed a preponderance of boys over girls displaying restlessness, destructiveness and aggression, while the situation was reversed for dependence and withdrawal.

IDENTIFICATION AND ASSESSMENT

Any discussion of the prevalence of handicap will inevitably raise the issue of identification. It has already been said that it is at times difficult to be precise about special needs in the early years, before children are challenged by the more intensive learning demands which the school makes. Identification, therefore, is often tentative and, perhaps for this reason, is not always carried out to the satisfaction of the parents.

The suspicion that something is wrong with children can arise at different times in their development. In cases of severe disability, it may be possible to make a diagnosis at birth. In other cases, while the medical team may fear that all is not well, the parents may have no knowledge of these fears; in yet other cases, the parents may be the first to become suspicious and have then to persuade doctors that investigations need to be carried out. The full extent of the handicap and its implications for the child's development are usually only gradually revealed, a situation which is particularly trying for parents who feel that they are constantly being made aware of more and more problems.

As the majority of births in Britain take place in hospital, medical personnel are immediately aware of a child with obvious congenital difficulties. Indeed, the baby may need special care very soon after birth. Opinions differ as to how the parents should be informed of their child's problems. In the authors' study,[2] for example, differences were apparent in the length of time taken before the parents were informed, although all professionals were agreed that it would be wrong to allow the parents either to worry about their children (if they had been taken into special care) for any length of time or to believe that they were normal if they had severe problems. In most cases, both parents were told together, although some paediatricians preferred to tell the father first, to gauge the effect the news would have on the mother.

The initial shock on being given the news is considerable. Parents speak of feeling stunned and being left speechless. Opinions as to future development are often more important to them than labelling the condition. As one parent in the authors' survey said, "I didn't know what 'mongol' meant and the explanation that the child had an extra chromosome didn't help at all. I wanted to know what would happen to her." Unfortunately, it is this forecasting of development which is difficult and medical personnel are often unwilling to commit themselves before they see how early development is progressing. This leaves the parents very apprehensive and the inability of doctors to be able to predict future development from examining very young children often sours the whole professional relationship. "Each time he sounds more pessimistic. I could murder him".[3]

Relationships between the medical profession and the parents are even more at risk when the handicapping condition is not immediately identifiable. Doctors and parents may be reluctant to voice their suspicions and both parties may feel that the other is concealing information. Lansdown[4] writes, perhaps rather extremely, of parents having to "battle with arrogant doctors, health visitors who know less about the handicap than they do and psychologists who hide behind a shield of professionalism" (p.4). While this situation is, hopefully, not typical, it still happens too often for comfort.

Identification, however, is only the first step in a long process of assessment. Affixing a label to a child is not only unacceptable, as has already been said, but also may give a false impression that the case has been dealt with. The "label" is only the basis for continuing discussion, particularly aimed at charting and encouraging the child's development in all possible aspects. In this process, information can be obtained from a variety of sources, including most importantly the parents' observations and the results of standardized assessments.

The importance of involving the parents in the assessment of young children has also been voiced by Newson[5] when she claimed that parents "are ignored in their expert role. A major resource for the people who are trying to find out about their children is wantonly wasted" (p.105). Parents may need help to observe their child's behaviour accurately and several schedules (see Appendix C) exist to provide the means of increasing their expertise, e.g. *PIP Developmental Charts* or the *Portage Checklist*. The PIP charts cover the skills developed by children in the first five years of life, grouped into five sections: physical development, social development, eye—hand development, development of play and language development. The format is clear and the scoring depends on whether or not the specified behaviour has been observed, e.g. "puts hands round cup when drinking". In a similar fashion, the Portage checklist covers easily observable behaviour, this time grouped into six categories: infant stimulation, socialization, language, self-help, cognitive development and motor development. In both instances, the list of items given offers guidelines as to what the next more advanced item of behaviour could be, thus providing working objectives for those concerned with the child. An advantage of assessing performance over all aspects of development is that it enables the child's strengths to be identified as well as weaknesses, thus offering clues to the working out of suitable programmes which will recognize what the child can and cannot do.

More complicated methods of assessment are available, such as the *Griffiths Mental Development Scales* or the collection of eighteen developmental tests devised by Wood. These scales, while covering the same major areas as those just described, namely motor, adaptive, language and personal—social, have to be administered by trained personnel and are too detailed and complex for general use.

With children of about 3 years of age upwards, information can be obtained from observation of their play. Such observation is particularly appropriate for young children who do not always respond well in any formal situation. Play also enables the parents to be fully involved in the assessment either as observers or as participants. Newson[6] shows ways in which play behaviours may be used to provide information on the child's ability to imitate, to follow instructions, to indulge in reciprocal play, to display fine and gross motor skills, to use speech or other means of communication and to show cognitive development. Toy libraries and the use made of them by parents and children are especially productive of information on development as developmental sequences can be discerned in the children's play with easily obtainable toys. The objective of all this observation is not simply to measure the stage the children have reached but to show in a systematic way how they are functioning, how they respond to situations which should be attractive to them and how they tackle the difficulties encountered. Observers should then be in a position to encourage and help in a really constructive way.

If children have low intellectual ability, they may need to be helped to play. Through play they develop imaginatively, socially, emotionally and cognitively. Indeed, it could be argued that play is even more essential for the handicapped child than it is for the non-handicapped. "Pretend" play is especially important as it encourages the child to think, to remember and, hopefully, to vocalize. Jeffree *et al.*[7] provide charts in their book as a framework for observing imaginative play and recording the child's progress in this area. Similar charts are provided for "skilful" play, "energetic" play and "social" play, along with a wealth of suggested play activities.

Teachers might find useful the *Effectiveness Motivation Scale* devised by Sharp and Stott.[8] This scale aims to describe competence in the nursery school or kindergarten environment. The teacher is asked to observe and rate the children's behaviour in eleven typical play settings, five concerned with individual play, five with social play and one with general mobility. Examples of the settings include building and constructing, make-believe games and talk with other children. Each group of descriptive items ranges from little or no evidence of the activity in question to good reaction to it or even over-reaction. Unlike the other assessments which have been discussed up till now, the Stott-Sharp scale produces numerical scores which can be interpreted by comparing any child's scores with the performance of the sample on which the scale was based. Scores are obtained for Effectiveness, Inconsequence (impulsiveness, disruptiveness) and Withdrawal. This scale is seen to be particularly useful in that it offers to the teacher an indication of children's ability to sustain and find enjoyable learning approaches involving curiosity and discovery which should stand them in good stead in the primary school's actively-based regime.

These examples illustrate the availability of more objective means of assessment than mere opinion. They make it possible for teachers and parents to express exactly in terms of quantity and quality the current level of functioning in the child being observed. The various scales are so devised as to enable the observations to be carried out quite naturally, a considerable advantage to any rater. They also enable the next step to be taken, for, just as identification of special needs should lead to full and precise assessment of them, so the assessment in turn should provide the basic information for building up a programme specifically aimed at helping to cope with these needs as effectively as possible. The question of programmes will be considered later in this book.

SUPPORT FOR PARENTS

It is not easy for a family to adjust to the special conditions created by a child with developmental difficulties of any kind. MacKeith[9] talks of feelings of inadequacy, of bereavement (at the loss of the normal child expected), of shock, of guilt and of embarrassment as well as biological reactions which may range from protectiveness to revulsion. Since it is known that such reactions are typical, it is surprising that support is not offered more often than it is, especially when so many different services are, or could be, involved with handicap. For the very young child with special needs, however, considerable gaps remain in the services offered, despite some enlightened attempts to bridge these gaps.

The medical and nursing services are the first to be involved with families with a child with special needs as it is their responsibility to identify the problem or confirm it. Where hospital-based specialists continue to monitor the child's progress, this is usually well received by the parents, the main criticisms being the brevity of the visits on occasion or the infrequent appointments. Not all specialists, however, are prepared to give the time necessary for parents to come to terms with the problem and may assume that, if the parents ask no questions, it is because there is nothing more they want to know. Much more likely, the parents' lack of response is a mixture of confusion, fear and awe, induced by the white coats, impressive buildings, strange terminology and a general impression of lack of time. Yet if the parents are not articulate enough to question the specialists, they may never find out essential information on the care or handling of their child or may base their reactions on misapprehensions. In most cases, parents would benefit from more sessions with specialists, especially in the early stages of diagnosis, where information could be repeated and explained and the parents' worries fully discussed.

One of the problems of suggesting the type of service which parents require at this time lies in the fact that two different kinds of counselling are required from the specialist. At one and the same time the specialist is expected to provide diagnosis (and discuss future development) and help the parents to come to terms with their own feelings. These two kinds of counselling call for different skills and it is unlikely that a busy paediatrician will succeed in both aspects. There would appear, therefore, to be room for another professional to take over some of this complex task.

The Warnock Report[1] suggested that this person might be the health visitor, who would come into counselling in the new role of the "named person" with particular responsibility for the young handicapped child and his parents. The Report envisaged a "named person" as providing "a single and constant point of contact for parents", seeing that their anxieties were followed up, putting them in touch with the supportive services and encouraging any opportunities for early education. The health visitor was originally selected for this role as she is the person who has responsibility for all young children in her area, but if she is to take on this counselling role *vis-à-vis* the family with a handicapped child, she will need some additional training. In the authors' survey, for example, it was shown that health visitors, teachers and playgroup leaders did not always agree on the identification of special needs. "The level of agreement as to whether the child had a problem or not was low ... In some cases, although children were identified by both respondents (health visitors and teachers/ playgroup leaders) as having a problem, the problem indicated was different ... There was a tendency for health visitors to say 'no problem' more often than the teachers and playgroup leaders."[2] Health visitors have very many fewer contacts with children than those who see them for a continuous period each day. They are perhaps, therefore, less aware of any difficulties the child may show, especially if these difficulties are in the areas of speech and behaviour, the two aspects in which difficulties have already been noted as being most common in pre-school children.

It would be unrealistic to expect any health visitor to be expert in all types of handicap. Yet the situation is such that she might well be faced with a child displaying a difficulty about which she might know less than the parents who are looking to her for information. Jacobs[10] comments on the strength of feeling among parents that information is not always available to them. His survey of severely physically and severely mentally handicapped children showed that 24% of the parents interviewed had had no contact at all with health visitors. However, it should also be said that 70% of those who had had contact found that contact helpful. The role of "named person" would call for considerably more time, and probably more expertise, than is presently available to parents, although it should be remembered that the number of children involved is, at most, one in five.

The family doctor, too, may find that he lacks full knowledge of some of the handicaps presented by children in his practice. Opinions appear to be divided among family doctors as to the nature of their role, if children's problems are sufficiently marked for them to be receiving clinical treatment. To some family doctors this means that the child has now become someone else's patient and they therefore wish at all costs to avoid interference. Parents often find this attitude hurtful and are disappointed when no enquiry is made about the progress of the handicapped child. Other family doctors regard their role as central and see themselves as co-ordinating the information which is coming in from a number of different specialist sources. In this, they are acting more like the "named person" previously discussed. The part which the family doctor should or could play is further complicated in group practices and many parents of handicapped children are daunted by the prospect of explaining to yet another doctor what their problems are, especially after a long wait with a difficult child.

A "constant burden" is how Margaret Voysey[11] described the presence of a child with developmental difficulties in the family group. It might, therefore, be expected that the Social Services would play an important part in helping the family to come to terms with the stresses and strains involved. Yet Social Service departments in some areas make a surprisingly small contribution to supporting the parents of children with special needs and that usually only when the family is facing further difficulties which threaten its survival. Where social workers were involved with families in the authors' survey, their help was appreciated but most families had had little contact with them. The Brighton survey[10] showed a similar result. Of mentions made of services which had helped the families in relation to the child's handicap, only 3.5% were of the social services. It would seem that social workers are seen more as a means of access to financial assistance than as potential counsellors. Yet if their job is to work with families under stress, very few families containing a child with special needs would fail to qualify for their help.

If education services are considered, gaps in the provision of support again become obvious. With the exception of hearing impaired children, and sometimes those with physical or visual problems, help is seldom offered prior to the age of 3 years, at which time children with special needs are considered for placement in a formal group. Parents are told to "stimulate" their child in the very early years, but the exact nature and timing of this stimulation is often not made clear or the reasons why it might be beneficial. It is in this area of planning early programmes to encourage the child's development that educational visitors to the home could offer a helpful service. In such a service, educational psychologists could play a significant part. There is a great deal that they could contribute to the educational development of the younger child, not just in identification and assessment but also in programme planning. Their support of any educational home visiting programme would, therefore, be invaluable. It is a pity that the size of their workload often prevents their full involvement with this age group.

Once the child attends an educational group, parents frequently turn to teachers for support. Most teachers are only too happy to comment on the child's educational progress but may show considerably more reluctance if any issues pertinent to his difficulty are raised. They often find it awkward to broach the subject of special needs with parents. They may also find it difficult to deal with specific queries from the parents or, indeed, to know what to expect from the child. As one teacher of an ambulant spina bifida boy in the authors' survey[2] said, "Lack of knowledge of potential meant that sometimes I confused inability and naughtiness, both ways".

With educational policy moving towards integrating children with special needs as far as possible in ordinary classes, more teachers are going to come into contact with these children. While teachers in special units for pre-school children have considerable expertise in dealing with special needs, the teacher in the ordinary classroom lacks this and probably lacks also any experience of, or training in, handling children who display them. Therefore, not only do parents need support from a range of professionals, so too do the teachers. At the moment, however, such support is seldom forthcoming in the pre-school years, a gap which is especially noticeable in efforts to plan programmes for these young children. Where programmes are offered, they are usually in special schools or units, while the child in the integrated setting is likely to be involved only in the normal school regime.

Finally, consideration should be given to the support available from the voluntary organizations concerned with different handicaps. Such organizations offer a wide range of services to parents from the publishing of information sheets to the organization of playgroups. Yet in the authors' survey[2] only 37% of the families interviewed were members of any organization. This is a rather lower percentage than was found in another survey[10] covering mentally or multiply handicapped children, but even there the number who had been in contact with any organization was only 54% and these would be parents of children about whose handicaps there could be little doubt. It appears that in the early years parents are reluctant to associate themselves with formal groups, often feeling that their child's handicap is not severe enough to warrant such association or not realizing the support they could obtain from membership.

What picture of handicap in the early years emerges from this overview? It must be admitted that it is rather a depressing one. Often special needs are not recognized formally until some considerable time has passed. Even when needs are identified, the situation may well not be made clear to parents, who are left without the support they need at a particularly trying time. Special programmes are seldom drawn up and implemented in the first years of life.

Some of the most imaginative and practical help has come from parents themselves. A number of voluntary organizations, for example the Down's Baby Association, make a link between parents as soon as a new instance is known. For older children, Kith and Kids[12] presents opportunities for self-help in socialization and in the development of play activities, the organization growing in the first place out of the absence of professional support, although it would not have developed as well as it did without the involvement of child psychologists.

Over the past years, parents have increasingly shown their ability to assist in the early education of their children as well as in their care. They have not only helped to pass on information on services available, they have also taken part in assessment, programme planning and the carrying out of such a programme. If such a contribution can be made in some parts of the country, it can be made in others. Parents may need guidance on how to cope but, given such help, they are able to provide considerable assistance for their children in the best possible setting, the home. Once parents have gained such expertise in the handling of their young child, they should be well suited to offering practical help in the continuing education of the child in a formal group.

Perhaps the most depressing facet of the whole discussion is the fact that the same comments have been made many times before. In the Glasgow report to the Carnegie United Kingdom Trust[13], the remark is passed that many of the adverse comments it contained had been made in 1917 in a previous report to the same body. The report concludes by saying, "It is clear, however, from this survey that the needs of the handicapped child and his family are not being met" (p.224). Precisely the same remark would be relevant to Jacobs' survey in 1977 and to the authors' own research in 1980. Where parents have achieved a breakthrough, they have done it despite bureaucracy. Their potential contribution to their child's development has still not been fully recognized and continues to be seen in many cases as ceasing once the child starts school. Of all times when a gap in services can be least tolerated, it is in the early years. At least there are now available, sometimes from professionals and sometimes from the parents themselves, some ideas as to how that gap might best be filled.

REFERENCES

1. DEPARTMENT OF EDUCATION AND SCIENCE (1978), *Special Educational Needs: Report of the Committee of Enquiry into the Education of Handicapped Children and Young People* (The Warnock Report), London: HMSO.
2. CHAZAN, M., LAING, A., SHACKLETON BAILEY, M. and JONES, G. (1980), *Some of Our Children*, London: Open Books.
3. LAING, A.F. and JONES, G. (1979), 'Discovery of handicap,' in LAING, A.F. (ed.) *Young Children with Special Needs*, Department of Education, University College of Swansea.
4. LANSDOWN, R. (1979), "The handicapped child and the parent: a consideration of the Warnock Report," *Education for Development* Vol. 5, No. 3, 4—10.
5. NEWSON, E. (1976), 'Parents as a resource in diagnosis and assessment,' in Oppé', T.E. and Woodford, P. (eds.) *The Early Management of Handicapping Disorders*. Elsevier: IRMMH
6. NEWSON, E. (1979), 'Play-based observation for assessment of the whole child,' in Newson, J. and E, *Toys and Playthings*, Harmondsworth: Pelican.
7. JEFFREE, D.M., McCONKEY, R. and HEWSON, S. (1977), *Let Me Play*, London: Souvenir Press.
8. SHARP, J.D. and STOTT, D.H. (1976), *Stott-Sharp Effectiveness Motivation Scale Manual*, Windsor: NFER.
9. MacKEITH, R. (1975), 'The feelings and behaviour of parents of handicapped children,' in Spain, B. and Wigley, G. (eds.), *Right from the Start*, London: NSMHC.
10. JACOBS, J. (1977), 'Improving communications between health service professionals and parents of handicapped children: a case study,' *Br. J. Ment, Subnorm.*, 23, 54—60.
11. VOYSEY, M. (1975), *A Constant Burden*, London: Routledge and Kegan Paul.
12. COLLINS, M. and COLLINS, D. (1976), *Kith and Kids*, London: Souvenir Press.
13. Carnegie United Kingdom Trust (1964), *Handicapped Children and their Families*, Dunfermline: Carnegie UK Trust.

2

PARENTAL INVOLVEMENT

Throughout its report, the Warnock Committee underlines the importance of the role of parents in the care and education of children with special needs, particularly in the early years. The Report regards parents as full partners in the educational process, and emphasizes that they should receive encouragement, advice and support to enable them to help their children effectively. Some aspects of the parental role have already been touched upon in the preceding chapter, but the nature of this role and the demands on parents of children with special needs will be examined more fully here. The varied kinds of programme available for parents will also be considered, and the chapter will conclude with a discussion of the ways in which home and school can collaborate.

THE PARENTAL ROLE

In many ways the role of parents of children with special needs is not very different from that of other parents. However, parents of children with significant disabilities do have a more complex and demanding role. Many mothers of "normal" under fives, even though they may obtain considerable satisfaction from motherhood, suffer from fatigue, frustration and depression. It is hardly surprising, therefore, if the stresses and strains arising from having a child who presents problems of some kind add greatly to personal and family tensions, especially while the child is at home all day. Even in the case of a mild handicap, parents may be extremely worried about the implications of the disability for the child's upbringing and general development. A full understanding of the special needs of children is not possible without insight into the emotional and social needs of their parents.

The functions and responsibilities of parents of under fives with special needs include:

ensuring the physical care and safety of their children;
giving them the experience of warm, affectionate and consistent relationships;
extending their social awareness;
providing appropriate stimulation and encouraging positive attitudes to learning and exploration.

In considering these functions and responsibilities it should be borne in mind that, while fathers are increasingly participating in the home routine, the main burden of child-rearing still falls on the mother. Research on the role of fathers has been so scanty that we know little of the extent to which their role in the family has changed in recent years. However, the involvement of the father is particularly important when there is a handicapped child in the family. A supportive father can make all the difference to the emotional and physical state of a mother struggling to cope with a young handicapped child. It is essential, therefore, that professionals should do whatever they can to encourage and involve fathers as well as mothers in discussions about a child and in any action that is suggested.

Providing physical care

Providing adequate physical care and ensuring safety may, in a number of cases, impose a considerable strain on the conscientious parent. For example, a cerebral palsied child may be difficult to move, or a hyperactive toddler may drive his parents to distraction by his inability to settle down to anything for more than a few seconds. In addition, the parents of severely handicapped children are likely to have to make frequent visits to hospitals or clinics. Parents in such situations need a good deal of psychological and material support. Parents living in socially disadvantageous conditions are less likely than others to seek all the benefits to which they are entitled, whether medical or financial. An initiative is often required on the part of the health visitor or social services to give them information on the assistance that is available, and to encourage them to take full advantage of such help.

Meeting emotional needs

Recent work on young children has tended to focus on the part played by family and group experiences in their cognitive and linguistic development. This emphasis has been a valuable one in that it has encouraged attention to be given to previously neglected areas, but the importance of social and emotional development should not be minimized: considerable evidence exists to indicate that the lack of loving and dependable relationships is likely to have an adverse effect on children's overall development. If they do not have satisfying relationships, not only will they suffer emotionally and socially but they may well find it difficult to live up to their intellectual potential in school, since adequate motivation and emotional stability are crucial factors in scholastic achievement.

In our society, it is the parents who provide a secure and affectionate base for the child. In most cases, they succeed in this function, sometimes in the face of severe difficulties such as living in poverty or in grossly unsatisfactory housing conditions. However, many parents of children with special needs, even when they have no financial or domestic worries, find it difficult to be as warm and loving towards their children as they would like to be. Their inhibition stems partly from their anxieties and feelings about themselves, and partly from their failure to obtain sufficient feedback from their children.

Almost inevitably, parents who perceive their children as different in significant ways from "ordinary" children feel anxious and worried. They are likely to feel uncertain about their own role in the causation of the handicap or in their handling of the child. They may have strong feelings of guilt, and blame themselves for not having a child who is "normal" in every way. Such negative feelings will prevent them from giving the child the degree of warmth and affection which is essential. To some extent at least, the child will experience rejection, though this may not be openly expressed. Rejection can take many forms, including overprotection or an undue measure of parental self-sacrifice, ostensibly in the interests of the child. Even where the parents of a handicapped baby start off with a loving attitude, they may gradually cease to provide stimulation of any kind if development is so slow that the child fails to respond to the attention given. Too often, parents give up just at the time when they might be rewarded by some positive response from the child.

If parents are to meet the basic emotional needs of their children, they will require the kinds of support discussed in Chapter 1. They will benefit from an awareness that their feelings are natural, and shared by many other parents in similar situations. Above all, professionals coming into contact with children with special needs should avoid adding in any way to the parents' feelings of guilt and self-reproach, but rather do what they can to encourage positive attitudes.

Extending social relationships

From a very early stage, the social development of children is greatly enhanced by the opportunities provided by their parents for them to have contact with other children and to extend their knowledge of the world outside the home. Some parents of handicapped children are reluctant to expose themselves and their child to the external world, fearing what other people might say. It is very important that children with special needs should, as far as possible, develop their awareness of other children and adults, and parents should not seek to hide them away from the world outside. Where they exist, mother and toddler groups can provide a good initial base for the extension of social relationships. At a later stage, the nursery school or playgroup can do much to reduce a sense of isolation on the part of both parent and child. Additionally, parents should, as far as is practicable, endeavour to take the child on appropriate outings and seek to involve the child in everyday activities such as shopping.

Providing appropriate stimulation: parents as educators

Studies of young children, including research involving disadvantaged families, have indicated that early childhood education should be thought of as involving parents as much as teachers.[1,2] There are a number of reasons for this, especially: (i) the family is the major socializing influence on the child; (ii) nursery schooling or playgroup participation, when it occurs, plays only a small part in the life of under fives; and (iii) the good home provides the young child with many of the experiences he needs for his cognitive and affective development.

Bruner[3] has stressed that intellectual development depends upon a systematic and rewarding interaction between a tutor and a learner, and there appears to be no real substitute for the "tutoring" provided by the parent on a one-to-one basis. Close interaction between parent and child, enhanced by a loving relationship, provides a unique basis for the acquisition of language skills and the understanding of concepts. The parents of the child who is developing normally do not need to make an excessive effort to fulfil their role as educators: the child learns naturally from daily experiences.

The parents of many handicapped children are in a different position. Apart from their need to adjust emotionally to the situation in which they find themselves, they have to learn skills additional to those involved in normal child-rearing. Feeding and dressing a physically handicapped child may present severe difficulties, and training the child to do things for himself even greater problems; encouraging a mentally retarded child to use language involves a great deal of time and energy. Parents obtain a high degree of satisfaction from even limited success in such efforts. However, they may not always be rewarded with any response from the child, or they may find that progress is extremely slow. They need to take care not to make excessive demands on the child, while trying to judge what step forward the child might be able to make.

It is important to recognize that, while parents and teachers have much in common in providing the kind of stimulation from which the child can benefit, the educational role of parents and nursery staff differs in fundamental ways, particularly in respect of skills and emotional involvement. Specific training gives the professional confidence in dealing with children, whereas the parent often feels insecure and something of an amateur, not only as an educator but often in child-rearing generally. Further, the close emotional involvement of parent with child, which enhances natural and incidental learning, tends to get in the way when parents try to assume a deliberate teaching role. Few parents do not become irritable in the course of a planned "tutoring" session. Teachers are in a better position to be objective, to stand back a little, and to avoid becoming emotionally upset at a child's failure to respond.

Parents of handicapped children are naturally anxious to see some discernible progress and are usually ready to make their contribution to this end. It is all too easy for them to become so involved in their educational role that this interferes with the emotional relationship between parent and child. Anyone involved in parent-involvement projects needs to be fully aware of the delicacy of their task and of the importance of understanding the attitudes and feelings of parents.

PROJECTS INVOLVING PARENTS

As already emphasized, many parents of children with special needs want to do something positive to help their children's development. However, without skilled advice they may be ineffective or even act in ways which are harmful: it is never easy to judge at what level a child is functioning or is capable of functioning and never easy to decide what the next step should be in a developmental programme. Children may either be set impossible tasks or be kept at a level where they do not face any real challenge. Consequently, over the years a variety of projects have been launched in order to provide parents with practical guidance and support. These projects have been directed mainly at parents of young children, on the grounds that it is highly desirable to give help at as early a stage as possible.

A wide range of approaches have been adopted in these projects, which may seek: (a) to impart to parents certain specific skills in teaching or training their child (e.g. dressing, toilet-training, using language); (b) to give them an intellectual understanding of the child's developmental needs; or (c) to focus on the parents' own feelings and attitudes.

Projects may seek to involve parents on an individual basis or in groups, and may aim to work mainly within the home or in other settings (clinics, workshops, toy libraries, school or playgroup). They will be discussed here under two headings: home-visiting schemes and group approaches.

Home-visiting schemes

For a variety of reasons, many parents are unwilling or unable to participate in activities arranged for them in clinics or other centres. Some parents will not make the effort required to attend such centres, some are unable to afford the cost of travel or have responsibilities at home which they cannot leave. Some, too, feel uncomfortable at the idea of joining a class or workshop, and are inhibited from attendance by their apprehension. For all such parents, home visiting with an educational purpose may be an effective strategy, and has the additional advantage of reaching the parents through the child in their own familiar environment.

Apart from peripatetic home teaching services for children with impaired hearing, organized by many local authorities, most of the home-visiting schemes launched in Britain have been concerned with socially disadvantaged children rather than with those handicapped in other ways. However, the Portage *Guide to Home Teaching* is being increasingly used with mentally and physically handicapped children.[4]

Schemes for disadvantaged children

Early home-visiting programmes, which were pioneered in the USA, tended to focus directly on the child rather than on the parents, but later projects aimed at stimulating interaction between mother and child and raising the morale and self-esteem of the parents. As Bronfenbrenner[5] has stressed, the key elements of successful intervention with socially dis-advantaged families are the involvement of parent and child in verbal interchange of a challenging nature and the existence of a mutual and enduring emotional attachment between child and adult.

Since 1970, when educational home visiting was intro-duced into Britain as part of the Educational Priority Area action-research project in the West Riding, a number of schemes have been launched by local education authorities, using professionals (usually health visitors or teachers), or by voluntary agencies. The usual practice is for the educational visitor to pay a regular weekly visit to the home, lasting about an hour, taking toys, games and books. The visitor tends to focus on helping the parents to foster the child's motor, linguistic, cognitive and social development. In most cases, families within a particular school cachment area are visited, to avoid labelling certain families as "deprived", though some independent agencies concentrate on multi-problem families.

It is not easy to assess the value of home-visiting projects aimed at reducing the adverse effects of social disadvantage on young children, but the results to date have been encouraging. The West Riding experiment illustrates some of the changes in attitudes and practices which a home visitor can assist in bringing about.[8] In this study, the need for help with language development soon became obvious: mothers would often anticipate the child's needs unnecessarily and the child's language was often restricted, particularly where there were other young children at home all day. The smaller and less-developed children were treated like babies because they looked like babies, and fewer demands were made on them. Surprisingly, few of the children had used "learning toys" by 21 months, but they soon found real pleasure in discovering new materials. The children involved in the experiment made definite gains in language, creativity and sociability. More important, however, than such gains was the change in the mothers' attitudes to the children's development and to their own role as parents. None of them had initially seen themselves as playing a vital role in their children's intellectual development, which they felt should be left entirely to the school; but once the mothers began to join in the children's activities, they saw how much they were teaching them, and they were anxious to go on helping. The child's obvious pleasure in the activities was the main factor in making the parents react favourably. Some of the parents were afraid of teachers and therefore not enthusiastic about approaching schools. These parents could all too easily be labelled as "apathetic" or "not interested", but their interest could be aroused with encouragement and support.

Donachy,[7,8] too, on the basis of controlled studies on mother—child interaction found that home-based programmes made mothers more aware of natural teaching opportunities in the course of the ordinary activities of the day and helped them to form better relationships with their children. On the basis of another project in Scotland (the Lothian Region Pre-School Educational Home Visiting Scheme), Raven[9] confirms that educational home visitors can have a marked effect on the attitudes of parents, who have unsatisfied educational and social needs. He emphasizes, however, that more thought should be given to the kind of qualities that we wish to see developed in children: the relative success of advantaged children may have more to do with the development of such qualities as initiative, independence and the tendency to question authority than with cognitive ability. Parents are in the best position to encourage these qualities, but it is extremely difficult for an outsider, without an extensive knowledge of the individual child, to show parents the "right" or "best" child-rearing practices.

Experiments over the past decade along the lines discussed above suggest that it is worth while persevering with parent education programmes based on the home. However, as Barbara Tizard[10] has pointed out, we still have much to learn about which aspects of young children's environment are significant for later scholastic achievement.

Schemes for mentally or physically handicapped children

In the case of children with serious mental or physical handicaps, the home visitor has to use a rather different approach from that required with socially disadvantaged children. While her help is likely to be welcomed, she will need rather more complex skills in "teaching" the child and progress will often be very slow. However, the Portage *Guide to Home Teaching*, devised in the USA, has proved a useful basis for home-visiting schemes for handicapped under fives.

The Portage programme is designed to help children who are functioning significantly (about one year or more) below their age level in physical, self-help, social, cognitive or communication skills. Initially a screening visit (or visits) is made by a home teacher, who sees the parents and child to establish rapport, answer queries and administer the Portage Developmental Checklist to determine eligibility for the programme and to obtain a base-line behavioural profile of the child. If the child is enrolled in the programme, the home teacher selects each week, with the aid of the parent, one or two "emerging" behaviours (i.e. where the child has mastered the necessary components of a behavioural item on the developmental checklist). Once a skill is chosen, the home teacher refers to the *Curriculum Guide* for suggested methods to teach the skill. This Guide consists of a box containing a card for each step on the developmental checklist. Each card suggests activities which are likely to be helpful in teaching the specific skill in question; these suggestions are meant to serve as a "spring-board" helping teacher and parents to develop additional ideas. The activities are not stated as behavioural objectives: the user must set up the suggestions in the form of specific objectives relevant to the child she is teaching. The child's learning style and coping behaviours are continuously observed, and the pace of the programme is adapted to needs and to the response given to the teaching.

The home teacher plans and writes up one or two "activity charts" for the coming week. After a week, she returns to evaluate the child's progress on the activity by taking post-baseline data, and makes further suggestions in the light of her findings. Although the programme gives very specific advice and is based on behaviour modification principles, it gives considerable flexibility to both teacher and parents. In addition to her educational function, the home teacher tends to become involved in discussing family and other problems with the parents and in advising them where to seek help with these problems.

Successful use of the Portage programme is reported by the Wessex Health Care Evaluation Research Team[11] and by the South Glamorgan Home Advisory Service.[12] The Wessex team found that parents co-operated well in the project, whch was designed to help mentally handicapped under fives. Relationships between mother, child and home-teacher remained pleasant, and specific task-centred activities were implemented on a very high proportion of all visits. The Wessex study, while suggesting that many components within the total package might be changed, confirmed the value of the Portage approach. This is supported by the South Glamorgan service, which is functioning smoothly even without extra resources being made available. The service caters for a wide range of children with developmental delay and is popular with referring agencies, both because it enables them to meet the parents' need for practical help and because the procedures are well specified. The families involved continue to make positive comments about their participation in the scheme, which is supported by a multi-disciplinary team.

Group approaches

Parents of children with special needs will usually be most receptive to advice on an individual basis, relating to their own child, rather than to guidance of a more general kind. However, group meetings have a number of advantages. They are economical in time and resources; they provide an opportunity for parents to share their problems with others and to realize that their situation is far from unique; and they encourage the pooling of knowledge about successful ways of coping with specific handicaps. Group instruction and discussion can also help parents to get the most out of the literature that is available for them.

Workshops

Group instruction in Britain has, in the main, taken the form of workshops for parents of mentally handicapped children. Cunningham and Jeffree[13] discuss the organization and structure of such workshops, consisting, in their case, of a tutored group of parents (maximum eight to ten), who came together for a series of 2½ hour sessions (about fourteen in all). They stress the importance of training parents, perhaps with the aid of developmental charts (see page 110), to observe the child in order to obtain a detailed picture of his strengths and weaknesses, or of his behaviour problem. This observation leads naturally into a discussion of aims and objectives, and a consideration of how any task should be broken down (task analysis). The parents try out the principles and techniques taught them, largely along behaviour modification lines, and implement them in their own homes. Cunningham and Jeffree found parents to be very co-operative and willing to persevere, and concluded that they benefited from the workshops. However, they stress that if a workshop course does not give parents what they want, it might do more harm than good.

Callias and Carr[14] describe how psychologists involved

groups of parents of severely subnormal children in behaviour modification programmes over a period of 2½ years. The methods of training focused on practical skills and techniques in relation to each parent's individual problems. The principles of behaviour modification were taught only incidentally in most cases, but more explicitly to the parents of children with multiple handicaps or problems, so that they would be able to apply these principles generally. Direct instruction and modelling in a variety of settings were used in preference to manuals or other materials, although treatment programmes were sometimes specially written. Callias and Carr concluded that it was possible to train parents in behaviour modification skills with a fair degree of success. Neither social class nor the mental health of the parents was related to the outcome of the programmes undertaken, but the frequency and length of contact were important factors. It was found difficult to break off contact with the parents involved in the programmes.

Therapeutic groups

Groups have also been set up with primarily therapeutic rather than educational aims, usually by child psychiatric units or psychological services. For example, Bentovim[15] describes work with parents' groups which formed part of a day centre for disturbed young children at the Great Ormond Street Hospital for Sick Children, London. Each day parents bringing their children to the centre met one of the psychiatric social workers for a group session lasting 45 minutes. Although these groups were set up initially to discuss practical problems, they became increasingly therapeutic in nature. In discussing their shared difficulties, parents both supported and confronted one another with their stresses and strains, frustrations and feelings of isolation.

HOME—SCHOOL COLLABORATION

Parents of young children with special needs feel a considerable sense of relief when the child is first admitted to school. Even the most competent and caring parents are supported by the knowledge that the child is in expert hands for part of the day, and that their own responsibility for the child is shared with others. The parents of the more severely handicapped children are usually particularly pleased that the child is considered able to benefit from attendance at school. In shedding some of their responsibility, the majority of parents are anxious to do what they can to support teachers in their task, and the benefits of involving parents in the work of the school are substantial. Home—school links help to ensure that the child is handled in a consistent way, and that there is continuity in the treatment received in different environments. A good relationship with their child's teacher can encourage parents to be aware of the part that they can play in the educational process and to improve their skills in observing the child and offering challenging tasks. Parents can also obtain much support from discussing their particular problems with the teacher, who can if necessary refer them to other agencies for appropriate help. In return, teachers can, through contact with parents, learn much about the children in their care which will be of value in planning individual programmes; they may also receive practical help from the parents in a variety of forms.

Difficulties in parent–teacher relationships

In spite of the obvious gains from a constructive partnership between home and school, barriers often exist on both sides which impede good relationships. Some parents are happy to "leave it all to the school"; some take a defensive stance, being apprehensive that they may be blamed for the child's difficulties or handicap; and others may be reluctant to "stir things up". A number of parents do not find it easy to talk to teachers. They may be uncertain of their own role in the child's development, or be afraid of showing a lack of knowledge or competence in a particular area. Socially disadvantaged parents may well feel a sense of inferiority in relation to teachers or other parents, who are perhaps better dressed or more articulate. Although most parents will soon overcome their initial inhibition, they will need a tactful and sympathetic approach if they are to become confident and natural in their contacts with the school.

Teachers, too, may be insecure in their relationships

with parents. They may be diffident about taking the initiative in discussing a child's problems, fearing a rebuff or a challenge to their authority; or they may not wish to upset the parents by suggesting that their child is being particularly difficult in class. Some teachers may think that, by virtue of their professional training, the handling of the child at school is their province and not the concern of the parents. However, those teachers who approach parents in a welcoming manner and a spirit of partnership are usually pleasantly surprised at the response which is forthcoming, even from parents labelled as "apathetic" or "indifferent".

No unanimity of opinion exists among teachers over such practices as the participation of parents in the classroom and home visiting.[16] Some teachers welcome parents in the classroom either as occasional visitors or as active contributors to class activities; others regard the presence of parents in the classroom as something of a nuisance and as possibly leading to conflict. With regard to home visiting, some feel that to visit a child's home is an intrusion and possibly detrimental to the parent—teacher relationship, while others consider that by making a personal visit to a child's home, they can gain in understanding of the family environment and also form a closer link with the parents.

A sensitive area

Home—school collaboration is certainly a very sensitive area but most of the difficulties likely to arise can be overcome by good will. Although some parents — especially the better educated ones — will show a keen interest in their child's schooling without being urged to do so, on the whole it is up to teachers to take the first step in encouraging parents to work with them to the best of their ability. Teachers themselves, however, need some guidance if they are to be fully aware of the contribution that parents can make, and if they are to possess the skills that are necessary in collaborating constructively with parents. To this end, the social and psychological services can contribute much by giving teachers the opportunity to attend in-service courses where, for example, interviewing and counselling techniques can be discussed. As appropriate, parents — fathers as well as mothers — might also participate in such courses.

CONCLUSION

This chapter has stressed that most parents of young children with special needs are very anxious to be involved in some way in their children's education and will respond positively to efforts made to encourage their active participation. It is obvious that a wide range of different forms of skilled support should be available to parents. During the early years, the one-to-one relationship between parent and child provides an excellent basis for cognitive as well as emotional growth, and parents may be as effective educators or therapists as professionals. However, without help they may not possess the requisite skills nor be fully aware of their own potential.

Although many considerations have to be taken into account in planning and implementing projects involving parents, certain general principles need to be borne in mind. Such projects should be guided by a sound knowledge of child development as well as of specific handicaps, and should seek to break down barriers often found in the expert—client relationship. Parents should be encouraged to take a positive attitude to their children, but not be given false hope, or be deluded into thinking that a child can be made normal where this is impossible. Considerable attention ought to be given to the establishment and maintenance of parental motivation. Both the content of programmes and the equipment used should be kept simple. Although some children require special equipment at home, complicated gadgetry should be avoided as far as possible, and materials which are easily available used to the fullest extent. Finally, it should never be forgotten that parents as well as children have individual needs, which are emotional and social as well as intellectual.

REFERENCES

1. HALSEY, A.H. (ed. 1972), *Educational Priority, Vol. 1: E.P.A. Problems and Policies*, London: HMSO.

2. CHAZAN, M. and WILLIAMS, P. (eds, 1978), *Deprivation and the Infant School*, Oxford: Basil Blackwell (for Schools Council).

3. BRUNER, J.S. (1966), *Towards a Theory of Instruction*, Cambridge, Mass.: Harvard University Press.

4. WEBER, S.J. *et al.* (1975), *The Portage Guide to Home Teaching*, Portage, Wisconsin: Co-operative Educational Service Agency.

5. BRONFENBRENNER, U. (1974), *A Report on Longitudinal Evaluations of Pre-School Programmes, Vol. 2 — Is Early Intervention Effective?* Dept. of Health, Education and Welfare, Washington, D.C.

6. SMITH, G. (ed. 1975), *Educational Priority: EPA, The West Riding Project*, London: HMSO.

7. DONACHY, W. (1972), 'Promoting cognitive growth in culturally deprived pre-school children', unpublished M.Ed. thesis, University of Glasgow.

8. DONACHY, W. (1976), 'Parent participation in pre-school education', *British Journal of Educational Psychology, 46, 31—39.*

9. RAVEN, J. (1980), *Parents, Teachers and Children*, London: Hodder & Stoughton (for SCRE).

10. TIZARD, B. (1975), *Early Childhood Education (a review and discussion of research in Britain)*, Windsor: NFER Publishing Co. (for SSRC).

11. SMITH, J., KUSHLICK, A. and GLOSSOP, C. (1977), *The Wessex Portage Project: a home teaching service for families with a pre-school mentally handicapped child (Parts I and II)*, Wessex Regional Health Authority: Health Care Evaluation Research Team.

12. CLEMENTS, J.C., BIDDER, R.T., GARDNER, S., BRYANT, G. and GRAY, O.P. (1980), 'A home advisory service for pre-school children with developmental delays', *Child care, health and development*, 6, 25—33.

13. CUNNINGHAM, C.C. and JEFFREE, D.M. (1975) 'The organization and structure of workshops for parents of mentally handicapped children', *Bull. Br. Psychol. Soc.*, 28, 405—411.

14. CALLIAS, M. and CARR, J. (1975), 'Behaviour modification programmes in a community setting', in Kiernan, C.C. and Woodford, F.P. (eds.) *Behaviour Modification with the Severely Retarded*, Amsterdam: Associated Scientific Publishers.

15. BENTOVIM, A. (1973) 'Disturbed and under five', *Special Education*, 62, 2, 31—5.

16. CHAZAN, M., LAING, A., SHACKLETON BAILEY, M. and JONES, G. (1980), *Some of Our Children*, London: Open Books.

3

EARLY EDUCATIONAL
EXPERIENCE (1)

It would be wrong to suggest that education is something
that happens only in formal groups and that the experiences
which the child has at home before joining such groups are
non-educative. In the first two years of life, the child achieves
a rate of learning which is never again reached and, moreover,
the learning accomplished then forms the basis for all subsequent learning. Early educational experience, therefore,
begins in the home and the quality of that experience is vital.

Bloom,[1] an American psychologist, has suggested why
this should be so, making in particular three points:

1 because change and development are so rapid in
   the early years, the experiences offered then have
   considerable impact on the child, much more so
   than they would have at a period when little
   alteration or development was taking place in
   the individual;
2 experiences are cumulative, inasmuch as development at any stage builds on prior development;
3 young children are seldom out of their home
   environments. They have, therefore, little opportunity to supplement inadequate experiences in
   the home with richer experiences elsewhere.

Adverse experiences in the early years can to some extent be
overcome in subsequent years, as the human learner is highly
flexible. Yet it must also be agreed that the overcoming of
adverse experiences at a later date is difficult for both pupil
and teacher.

Children with special learning needs are particularly

vulnerable in the very early years. Some of their development may be delayed, e.g. mobility or speech, and their difficulties may lead parents to curtail their experiences rather than extend them. Development is uneven and sometimes undue concentration on the child's difficulties may lead to a neglect of other areas of development where there may be the potential to approximate to normal development.

As yet, little by way of constructive help is offered in the very early years to parents of children with special learning needs. As discussed in Chapter 1, most support comes from paediatricians and health visitors and these tend to have a greater concern for the child's physical well-being than for educational progress. There is, also, the guidance given by local authority advisory staff in the case of certain handicaps, mainly defects of hearing or vision, and the opportunities present for meeting with others in the 'mother-and-toddler' groups for the under-threes. Educational home-visiting, that is, visiting with the specific intention of promoting the child's development, especially intellectual development, has been experimented with in a number of areas. The contribution which it can make towards helping parents of young, handicapped children has already been discussed in Chapter 2.

It might be expected that educational psychologists would contribute from their expertise to the education of young children with special learning needs. Despite the fact that their skills are very much in tune with this age group, surprisingly little contact seems to be made[2] and that usually only for assessment purposes prior to placement at the age of 3 years. The trend is, however, as was noted in Chapter 1, in the direction of early involvement by the psychologist with the child with special needs and his family. On the assumption that Bloom is right and that the early years are vital, the question arises of what experiences and opportunities should be offered in them. A further question is where such experiences and opportunities should be offered.

EDUCATIONAL EXPERIENCES

Let us consider five children: Joyce, Marie, Kathleen, Roy and Steven. All are children with special needs and all are nearly five years of age. Marie and Joyce were born with spina bifida; Kathleen and Roy are both severely mentally handicapped, and Steven has a moderate hearing loss.

In the case of Marie and Joyce, their problem was obvious at birth. Marie was operated on within seven days and a valve to control the gathering of fluid in the spinal cord was fitted. In Joyce's case a similar operation was performed but the baby had to be taken to a hospital in another town and did not come home until she was 30 days old. Both mothers had to go home without their babies and both found this an upsetting experience. In Marie's case, the doctor had placed so much stress on the gravity of the condition that her mother had resigned herself to the baby's dying, and she found it very difficult to adjust to the fact that the baby was going to survive but would be handicapped. Both children are incontinent and in wheelchairs.

Kathleen weighed just over three pounds at birth and developed pneumonia in the first days of life. She was placed in an incubator for five weeks. Nothing was said about her subsequent development but her mother began to worry about this when Kathleen was about 16 months old. Her language was very slow to develop, she was late in walking and feeding herself and was not toilet trained until she was three years old. At 4 years 6 months, she has only eight clear words.

Roy was born after his mother had had a threatened miscarriage. He was taken into intensive care for a day but after that was treated as normal and returned home at the usual time with his mother. He was examined at the local clinic at 11 months and his mother thought she heard someone mutter that he was subnormal but nothing was said to her. At the age of 15 months he saw a specialist about his eyes as he has a squint and he was referred to a paediatrician by the specialist. The mother was then told that the child was mentally handicapped, a diagnosis she found hard to believe despite admitting that Roy was slow to walk and to talk. His language is still very poor and, in addition, he is hyperactive, destructive and incontinent.

Both of Steven's older brothers are partially hearing and doctors were therefore alert to the possibility that he might be too. Before Steven was a year old, high frequency deafness in one ear was diagnosed. His mother and father are separated with the father looking after the three boys and their sister, so that things are not easy at home. Steven should wear a hearing aid at all times.

The first thing which becomes obvious from any consideration of these five children is that their problems are not easily categorized. Similar problems may be displayed or the same label attached to the condition but the individual differences in, for example, the parents' ability to cope, are marked. In some cases, the medical profession has dealt well with the family and the problem; in other cases, there would seem to be room for improvement.

What sort of educational opportunities do these children need to have? To begin with, all of them place a considerable burden on their parents, however well that burden may be shouldered. The parents, therefore, need first of all to be given considerable information and help so that, in the bewildering early years when the implications of the handicap start to become clear, they can aid their child's development from the very beginning. Obviously it is going to be difficult to enable parents to see how they can help if they refuse to accept the child's handicap. The need for careful diagnosis and specific advice and guidance for the future has already been noted in Chapter 1. If the educational opportunities of the early years are not seized, the chance may never present itself so easily again.

Children with special needs more often than not have language difficulties, showing problems in their receptive or expressive language or both. It is particularly important that parents should stimulate the early beginnings of language, say in babbling, so that the child hears sound used in a responsive way and gets the feeling of the 'give and take' of communication. These children are often slow to talk and parents may become disheartened when so little progress is made and words never seem to become established. It is particularly important that parents should not abandon their efforts. Only by persevering will progress be made eventually and even if the children do not succeed in uttering actual words, they will still benefit from being part of a communication system instead of being handled in silence.

Self-care skills also have to be established if at all possible. Without making the situation into a battle of wills, parents should try to encourage any moves which children make with respect to feeding themselves or undressing themselves or keeping themselves clean. A lot of praise and affection is needed for any indication that these skills may be emerging. The acquisition of these skills is educational in the widest sense and vital for subsequent adjustment to school.

There is a temptation in the early years to keep children with special needs isolated from their peers. Mothers may feel upset or embarrassed to see their handicapped child with non-handicapped children and yet young children do need to become accustomed to being with others. One other child may be enough to begin with. All children have to learn social interaction skills as anyone watching the "play" of two young children will quickly realize. It may take children with special needs a little longer to accept others or they may need more supervision and help than usual but again their future response to formal groups will be considerably facilitated by their having become accustomed to other children before the age of 3 years.

When children with special needs do enter a formal group, their educational opportunities increase. Whatever the type of provision (see Appendix B) and whatever the nature of the child's difficulties, educators of young children would give their aims as being the development of social/emotional and intellectual skills, the promotion of links between home and school and the encouragement of the aesthetic aspects and physical well-being of the children in their care.[3] How much children with special needs require in these areas can be seen from further examination of the five children already described.

For Marie and Joyce, their handicap is mainly in the area of physical development. If they can get into the nursery in their wheelchairs, they can probably benefit from much of the programme on offer. Their motor skills are, of course, seriously impaired but in both these cases there is not much evidence of any accompanying severe mental handicap and both appear to have low average mental ability. The main danger facing them is that they may be "babied" by the others in the class who may do things for them that they could easily do for themselves.

Kathleen and Roy present a very different picture in any nursery setting. Their learning difficulties are marked and they still need to acquire the skills that most children will have developed before the age of 3. Roy, for example, is not yet toilet trained, both are poorly co-ordinated and both have minimal language skills. They require special pro-grammes to help them acquire or develop these important self-care skills. Any future educational progress, for example, success in pre-reading skills, will depend on their ability to deal adequately with language and Roy in particular needs to learn how to get on with other children.

Steven's problems require a different solution. His home was in fact visited by a peripatetic teacher of the deaf who had given advice to his father on suitable stimulation for the boy at regular intervals since Steven was 18 months old. One of the main difficulties is that the father has little time to implement these suggestions as he is overburdened with the responsibility of looking after four children, three of them with hearing loss. Steven, therefore, needs an educational setting where he can be given a considerable amount of individual attention and where a teacher of the deaf and a speech therapist will together plan an individual programme for him.

Looking, however briefly, at these five children serves to emphasize that a number of different professionals, paediatricians, speech therapists, physiotherapists, specialist teachers, social workers and educational psychologists, should be involved in working with them both before and after school placement. There would, indeed, appear to be a gap in the services offered in the years before three, where an edu-cational home visitor might be invaluable in offering continu-ous guidance as to how to maximise the child's potential so that every educational opportunity is seized.

EDUCATIONAL PLACEMENT

What form of nursery provision is being offered to these five children? Interestingly enough, all are in some form of pro-vision which would indicate that the consensus of opinion is that these children benefit from contact with others and need to be helped outside the home setting at a fairly early age. It may also be that an easier transition to formal schooling at the age of 5 is envisaged if they have this prior experience of being with other children.

Marie and Kathleen are both in ordinary nursery schools. Despite a rather unsuitable classroom, as it has different floor levels, Marie manages well. Her teacher has arranged ramps in appropriate places and she has no great difficulty in moving her wheelchair about. She is making good progress and her mother is very pleased with the placement. Kathleen has much greater difficulties in her school. She has been seen by an educational psychologist since her admission and he has confirmed that she has very low intellectual ability. Her lack of speech presents barriers to interaction with her teacher and with her peers. She has not as yet been seen by a speech therapist. It is doubtful whether any teacher in an ordinary nursery could cope with the problems which Kathleen presents and these seem to be magnified by the fact that her nursery is "open plan", offering little opportunity for quiet, individual language work were such a programme planned.

Joyce is in the nursery unit of a special school for the physically handicapped. She, like Marie, is making good progress and her mother, too, is pleased with the placement. The question of ordinary school placement was never raised before she entered the special unit, the arrangement being made, with the mother's full consent, by the Community Medical Officer and the Headmaster. Her mother visited the unit before Joyce was admitted and was very impressed by it even although Joyce has to travel twelve miles each day by local authority transport.

Roy is in an ordinary playgroup. It was felt that he was not yet ready for a nursery placement but would benefit from occasional sessions spent with other children. He attends for two hours twice a week and his mother has to stay with him, as his behaviour is often uncontrolled and he may be a danger to other children. The premises are not entirely suit- able, the group meeting in a rather gloomy church hall with a high ceiling and little storage space. The group leader shows considerable initiative in planning activities and the mothers are keen to play their part, but Roy's presence does demand a considerable amount of their attention. The group leader is a trained nurse and, as it happens, none of the mothers who help has any experience of teaching. It would probably be true to say that Roy is only just being contained in the group setting.

Perhaps because of his family history and background, Steven was placed in a partially hearing unit. He is the only under-five in the group, the next youngest child being nearly seven years of age. He shows good co-ordination but his expressive language and his comprehension are poor. His teacher is working on these areas, but her work might have been easier had Steven had some companions of his own age with whom he could play. As it is, he is a solitary, little boy who is no trouble to anyone but appears somewhat lost.

It is easy to speculate on whether or not the provision offered is the best possible. In practice, children are often placed where there is space available. The ideal would be different. What is required is full discussion by everyone concerned, including the parents, and careful follow-up of all placements to assess their success. Where no firm decision can be taken, placement in an assessment unit or an observation class may allow time for more detailed review although such placement is only temporary and may cause the child to have to make an additional adjustment at an early age.

One of the most difficult decisions to take is whether or not a child with special needs should be placed in an ordinary group. This problem will be looked at in more detail towards the end of the chapter, once the range of facilities available in the various forms of provision and the support offered to the staff in them have been discussed.

FACILITIES FOR UNDER FIVES WITH SPECIAL NEEDS

A study by the authors[8] showed that some children with special needs were facing considerable problems with regard to facilities if placed in an ordinary school environment. Toilets were at times some distance away or stairs had to be climbed to reach them, there were uneven surfaces in the classrooms and a considerable rake on the playground. Facilities for washing children in privacy were not good, and schools or units often lacked separate rooms for interviewing parents, withdrawing children or holding medical inspections. Nursery and reception class staff had come to accept these difficulties in many cases and sometimes had developed ingenious ways of coping, but there is an obvious necessity for adequate facilities before children with special needs are placed in ordinary classrooms. It would seem that such placement is sometimes done without full consideration being given to the conditions prevailing and without the necessary alterations being made.

Special schools and units had much more by way of special facilities, not surprisingly as many of them were purpose built. Even so, the staff were not always fully satisfied with the facilities, and a number of useful alterations could have been made with regard to positioning of radiators, ease of access to other rooms and toilet facilities, especially for children in wheelchairs. In one school, entrance to the class-room was through a small kitchen and while staff were pleased to have such a facility, the layout of the rooms could perhaps have been more carefully thought out.

Playgroups, including those which accept children with special needs, probably have fewer amenities, especially large equipment, than other nursery groups, although the situation across the country is very variable. The main difficulty for the playgroups is that they usually operate in shared premises which often do not have direct access to outdoor play areas. They may not, therefore, have large apparatus such as climb-ing frames, slides or tricycles and, as a result, tend to con-centrate on smaller group or individual activities, such as painting, playing with puzzles or dressing up. As these latter activities are among the best for promoting cognitive and linguistic development, and in addition, there is a high pro-portion of adults to children, playgroups may well find that the restrictions in the range of their activities are not com-pletely without benefit to them.[4,5]

Other problems arise from the location of playgroups in premises which are not entirely suited to their purposes. Often, as in church halls, there may be plenty of space but the lighting or flooring may be poor for young children and apparatus usually has to be stored away at the end of each session. Nevertheless, information from the Child Health and Education Study[6] reveals few major differences between the institutions catering for young children by way of small equipment or activities generated by that equipment. Practic-ally all institutions had a book corner, dolls and prams, construction toys and a home corner, while almost all offered painting and crayoning, puzzles and listening to stories. Differences arise in the amount of time available for using the equipment and the way in which the choices are presented to the children.[7]

On the whole, staff seem to be willing to adjust to a variety of environments and to try to find ways around any problems set by the premises in which they have to work. Finding themselves with a rather steeply-raked playground, for example, they do not complain of its unsuitability or even danger for some children but rather see it as an ideal runway for small wheeled toys. Whether or not staff should have to regard environmental difficulties as a challenge is another matter. Given only modest sums of money, minor structural alterations, suggested by the staff themselves, could make a considerable difference to the smooth running of the groups. Environmental difficulties do not appear to prevent the admission of children with special needs on many occasions, but they do make successful working with these children just that much more difficult.

TEACHER/GROUP LEADER SUPPORT

Here a distinction can be made between ordinary schools, day nurseries and playgroups, and special schools, units or groups. The study mentioned above[3] showed that where contact had been established with outside agencies, it was most likely to have been in the special sector of education. Ordinary schools or groups received very little by way of outside support.

Within the special groups, support will, of course, vary depending partly on the type of difficulty catered for and partly on the relationships which have developed over the years. Thus the above study showed that schools for physically handicapped children and hospital schools had good access to speech therapists and occupational therapists, while units for children with sensory handicaps had frequent visits from specialist advisers. Educational psychologists were also involved in special education, most children being seen by them before placement and some being the focus of specially-planned programmes thereafter. Nevertheless, staff in special educational settings would have welcomed more contacts than they had, especially with doctors and social workers.

In the ordinary schools, teachers often felt ill-informed about the nature of the handicap and its implications. Medical details, for example, were hard to come by and this lack of knowledge caused considerable uncertainty as to what the child might or might not be expected to do. Discussion between parents and teachers certainly helped here, clarifying for both what the child had accomplished and might be encouraged to attempt, but in these circumstances it is only too easy to assume that certain activities are beyond the child's capacity. Were more precise details of the difficulties faced by the child known, it might be possible to see how they could be circumvented.

Teachers in ordinary schools, too, need guidance from those more experienced in dealing with special learning needs than they are, in the planning of programmes for individual children. Unless a full explanation of the specific needs has been given it may seem unduly burdensome to have to provide special work or different methods for one or two children. Without some help from others, teachers may well offer to children with special needs simply the normal nursery or infant programme. While this may be admirable for some aspects of the children's development, it is unlikely to help their specific difficulties which have been characterized as "special". Educational psychologists, organizers, advisory teachers and special school staff could all make a contribution towards offering immediate and continuing support to the staff of ordinary schools when pupils with special needs are admitted.

Day nurseries and playgroups may face particular difficulties in obtaining advice, especially if the child's special needs are in the intellectual, or cognitive, aspect of development. Emphasis in these groups is on the care of the children and on their social development. Playgroups function for only a rather brief period in the day and there may be little opportunity to work with a particular child as most of the experiences provided may be group-oriented. In the day nurseries, too, the practice of working in a close one-to-one relationship to achieve a particular, predetermined objective is often not well established. The Social Services departments who carry responsibility for the running of these groups are appointing members of their staff to take a particular interest in them, and it is to be hoped that they will liaise with their educational colleagues to ensure that the necessary experiences are provided for children with special needs.

SEGREGATION OR INTEGRATION

A great deal of argument has arisen as to whether children
with special needs should be educated along with other
children or whether their needs can best be met in smaller,
separate units staffed by adults who have had considerable
experience in dealing with particular needs. The discussion is
inevitably wide ranging and frequently imprecise, as so much
depends on what is meant by the term "special needs" and
as schools differ considerably. General agreement would
appear to exist, however, that no child should be placed in a
separate special school who could, with no detriment to himself or other children, be educated in the ordinary school.

Before any decision is taken to place a child with special
needs in an ordinary class careful consideration must be given
to several aspects. These include the special facilities which
such a placement may require (e.g. special ramps, toilets,
ground floor accommodation), the attitude of the staff to
such a placement and the weight of responsibilities they
already carry (e.g. numbers in class, availability of nursery
aides), and the effect of such a placement on the other
members of the class. If all of these pre-conditions were to be
satisfied, there still remain for consideration the special needs
which the child has and whether these can be adequately
coped with by the ordinary class teacher. Obviously, as has
already been said, the teacher is more likely to be able to
cope if she is well prepared for the placement, well informed
about the particular difficulties and well supported while the
child is in her class.

In the Warnock Report, a distinction is made between
locational, social and functional integration. In locational
integration, special units are attached to or adjoin ordinary
schools. Links between them may be very tenuous or fairly
close depending on the attitudes of the staff concerned and
the organizational arrangements made. Separateness, however,
remains, to a greater or lesser extent. Social integration leads
to a much closer relationship between ordinary pupils and
puils with special needs, inasmuch as the children share out-
of-class activities, playing together and perhaps taking meals
or attending assemblies together. Of course, how much genuine
integration occurs depends on the opportunities, and the
encouragement, offered for it to take place. The fullest form

of integration is functional integration, for here the pupils with special needs are part of the ordinary schools, working alongside the other children. There is thus a continuum of integration just as there is a continuum of need, and the best solution may be to try to provide for all of the different degrees of need with different kinds of provision.

The more severe the handicap or the more specialized the needs, the more difficult it is for the child to be placed in an ordinary class. Consideration of the case of physically handicapped children may help to illustrate the complexity of the decisions to be taken on placement. In a review[9] of such children's progress in special units attached to ordinary schools, five different categories of physical handicap were distinguished: children who have physical handicaps but who are mobile, continent and without special learning difficulties; more severely handicapped children but still with no special learning difficulties; children with mild handicap but with special learning difficulties; children with fairly severe physical handicap and substantial learning difficulties; and children with severe physical and severe mental handicaps. This categorization clearly shows the continuum of need which exists and, equally, points to the continuum of integration which is possible. While there may be nothing to prevent the first category of children from being most appropriately placed in local schools with only minor alterations in facilities or organization, the fifth category probably requires separate special schooling, even, in some cases, in residential schools.

With young children, however, there is every reason to expect the ordinary school or group to be capable of meeting many of their needs. The normal programme stresses language development and social development, both of vital importance to handicapped children. At the nursery stage, children may see fewer differences between themselves and others and some problems, for example of incontinence, are not in any way exceptional. Being carried or toileted or having speech difficulties are not unfamiliar to any of the children in the group. There is, therefore, a good argument for placing young children with special needs in ordinary settings prior to compulsory school entrance. With the latter, appropriate placement may have to be reconsidered as the special needs may inhibit progress when learning demands increase.

It is not only in Britain that the move towards integrating children who have special needs with ordinary children as far as possible is supported. Sweden showed itself a pioneer in this respect and Denmark is also following such a policy. In America, the Public Law 94—142 mandated equal education for the handicapped, this being interpreted as implying that the "least restrictive" environment should be provided for children with special needs; Canada, too, has similar legislation. It has been shown, of course, that integration in its fullest sense cannot be legislated for. To place a child with special needs in an ordinary classroom does not mean that he will be accepted as a full member of that classroom. Nor does legislation mean that the child's needs inevitably become paramount in decision taking. Parents in America have generated considerable litigation on the basis of the Public Law, some of it from over-inflated hopes of "normalization" and unrealistic estimates of their child's capabilities. Nevertheless, the move towards bridging the gulf between ordinary and special education which current thinking reveals is a hopeful one for the children concerned and their parents.

CONCLUSION

In this chapter consideration has been given to the different educational opportunities available for young children with special needs. The special unit may have superior facilities and the staff may be more experienced than in ordinary provision, but there are some disadvantages. Young children in particular may benefit from placement in an ordinary group where they can copy normally behaving children and experience a normal programme. On the other hand, as has been pointed out, the normal programme may not be sufficient for children's special needs and normal behaviour may be beyond their capabilities. In the long run, the question of whether to segregate children with special needs or to integrate them in ordinary education becomes a matter of discussion. Children's needs vary, even when the presenting handicap carries a similar label. The decisions have to be taken on the basis of the individual child's needs and in the light of the conditions existing in the group to be joined rather than on consideration merely of the label. The decisions must also be backed up with sufficient support for the staff concerned so that the child receives as valuable an educational experience as possible in the early years.

REFERENCES

1. BLOOM, B.S. (1964), *Stability and Change in Human Character-istics*, New York: John Wiley & Sons.

2. CHAZAN, M. (1979), 'Identification, assessment and treatment: the role of the educational psychologist', in LAING, A.F. (ed.) *Young Children with Special Needs*, Swansea: Faculty of Education.

3. TAYLOR, P.H., EXON, G. and HOLLEY, B. (1972), *A Study of Nursery Education*, Schools Council Working Paper 41, London: Evans/Methuen.

4. TURNER, J.F. (1974), 'Cognitive effects of playgroup attendance', *Irish Journal of Education*, 8, 1, 30—35.

5. BRUNER, J. (1980), *Under Five in Britain*, London: Grant McIntyre.

6. van der EYKEN, W., MICHELL, L. and GRUBB, J. (1979), *Pre-Schooling in England, Scotland and Wales*, Strasbourg: Council of Europe.

7. SYLVA, K., ROY, C. and PAINTER, M. (1980), *Childwatching at Playgroup and Nursery School*, London: Grant McIntyre.

8. CHAZAN, M., LAING, A.F., SHACKLETON BAILEY, M. and JONES, G. (1980), *Some of Our Children*, London: Open Books.

9. COPE, C. and ANDERSON, E. (1977), *Special Units in Ordinary Schools*, London: University of London Institute of Education.

4

EARLY EDUCATIONAL
EXPERIENCE (2)

How children with special needs will be received into nursery
or reception classes or playgroups clearly depends on the
individual child, the family background, previous experience
and the group the child is to join. Continuing success in a
group also depends on many things, including the effectiveness
of the programme offered and the relationships established in
the group. This chapter aims to look at a number of the
important factors involved in adjustment to early educational
experience, considering the first contacts which the child has
with formal groupings and subsequent progress.

THE MOVE FROM HOME TO SCHOOL

To move from a familiar situation in which one or two adults
provide concern and attention, often on a one-to-one basis,
to a strange setting in which there are many others competing
for toys and adult approval or help is not easy for any child.
Children with special needs may have particular difficulty if
their previous experience, for whatever reason, has not been
compatible with the school's expectations.

In any formal grouping, children have to show the ability
to work and play alongside, if not with, others, to share and
to co-operate and at the same time to look after themselves
and their possessions. To acquire these skills is often the main
reason why children attend nursery groups. Successful acquisition of these skills is, however, dependent on the extent to
which the children have begun to learn sociability and self-
care in the very early years prior to attendance. If certain
children, therefore, because of their physical or intellectual

limitations or their emotional problems, have become, for example, highly dependent on their parents and have seldom been encouraged to try to cope for themselves, they are at a considerable disadvantage on entry to a group. In a similar way, if they have had few contacts with other children, co-operation and even tolerance of others may be difficult for them.

Research evidence as to how young handicapped children settle in to the first formal group they encounter is scarce. Placement is likely to be more straightforward if the adults in charge of the group feel that they have some understanding of the children's special needs before admission so that they can plan appropriately. It is, therefore, essential that the parents, or someone who knows the child well, discuss the placement with the staff concerned and that the staff and child meet. Any discussion of special needs has to be as full and as frank as possible. It is not helpful for parents to gloss over difficulties or to suppress information, either favourable or unfavourable. Visiting prior to group entry is now a well-established practice and eases the children in to the new situation. As much information as possible on their routines, strengths and weaknesses needs to be given to the adults who will care for them in the group so that the children are not faced with tasks which may be too difficult or too easy for them. First impressions are important and a good start to group participation can only help to promote full integration.

It may be, however, that special needs become apparent only after entry to the group. For example, the extent to which a child lags behind in intellectual development may not be fully realized by his parents, especially if he is an only child or separated in years from any siblings. Whether or not such a child, or others whose special needs are diagnosed after group entry, will adjust to the group situation depends on many factors including, above all, the skill of the group leader in recognizing the difficulty and in being able to take the necessary action to deal with it, both in her own approach and in contacting others.

With regard to the general reaction of young children to school entry, the Plowden Report[1] investigated a sample of infant school starters, just over 200 children being involved. This investigation showed that, according to their teachers' assessments, about a quarter of the children exhibited some signs of distress on first parting from their mothers and that, of these, about twenty per cent were distressed for a month or more. Mothers, too, reported that just over a quarter of the children were distressed over school entry, although fewer reported prolonged distress over a month than the teachers had. It would appear, therefore, that it is fairly common for children to dislike parting from their mothers but that most settle in after a brief period of upset. More detailed investigation showed that those showing prolonged distress were often worried or fussy children, who were also behind the others in self-care skills such as doing up buttons or shoe-laces. They seem to be, therefore, as a group rather dependent on familiar adults and unsure of any new situation.

These findings were confirmed in another study[2] which also showed that boys were more likely to have difficulties than girls and that for a small proportion of children the difficulties first noted at school entry persisted over the infant school years. In particular, this study stressed that children who had problems in concentrating were likely to show poor adjustment to school and its demands. Their restlessness and inability to spend time constructively on any one activity led to behaviour which their teachers found disturbing and which also probably prevented their deriving full benefit from the school programme. Children with adjustment difficulties are children with special needs. The converse may also be true, namely that children with special needs are "at risk" of having problems in adjusting to school or to their first experience of formal groups because of the additional difficulties which they experience.

EDUCATIONAL NEEDS AND THEIR SATISFACTION

A child's educational needs cannot be considered apart from the general psychological needs of which they are specific instances. Kellmer Pringle[3] lists four general needs which all children have: the need for love and security, the need for new experiences, the need for praise and recognition and the need for responsibility. To satisfy these needs in young handicapped children is not easy as they may only too easily be "at risk" of rejection or over-protection by their parents. They may also be restricted in their ability to explore and discover, may seldom succeed in what they tackle either at home or in school and may even be deliberately shielded from attempting to take on the responsibilities appropriate to their age. It is also true that the handicap itself generates additional needs which the non-handicapped do not have.

Often it is once a child comes to join a group of other children that individual differences become obvious. Physically handicapped children, therefore, will need special arrangements made for them before they can function in the group environment. Structural alterations should be completed before one of these children join the group so that they are generally not made to feel more different than need be the case. Anderson[4] has emphasized that while the child whose handicap is of a non-neurological nature (e.g. heart condition, leg deformity) may be able to respond well to the normal nursery regime, the child with neurological impairment (e.g. cerebral palsy, some spina bifida conditions) usually has considerable attentional and perceptual difficulties which may well necessitate a special programme. Similarly, children with sensory defects may need special help if they are to make full use of any residual hearing or sight and not to begin to fall behind others in the group setting, where emphasis is placed on listening and looking.

The educational needs of mentally handicapped children are sometimes difficult to satisfy in the ordinary group. Because of intellectual limitations, progress is slow and much more frequent repetition and continuing practice are required. While they need intellectual stimulation as much as other children they find new ideas difficult to grasp and easy to forget. If the pace is slow enough, however, and the new material or experience carefully structured, they can make progress. At the nursery and playgroup stage, in particular, their problems of assimilation and understanding may not be so acute as they may be later, for there are plenty of opportunities to repeat activities and to progress at one's own pace.

The value of, for example, playgroup attendance can be seen in Turner's[5] study, where she shows that in a group of socially disadvantaged children who probably had linguistic difficulties, playgroup attendance led to a significant improvement in their vocabulary and in their reasoning ability. How much progress can be made by an intellectually limited child with linguistic difficulties depends, of course, on the nature and extent of these limitations, but encouragement to use language appropriately in a warm, supportive environment with interested adults can be of considerable help.

Staff have no difficulty in identifying aggressive, restless and destructive children or withdrawn children. Such behaviour problems stand in the way of the children's social development, the promotion of which is always recognized as being of prime importance in the early years. These children need help in learning how to establish better relationships with others so that they can benefit from the opportunities for companionship which attendance at groups offers. It may be that teachers will need to make contact with other professionals, such as educational psychologists, to help them to plan suitable approaches to managing these behavioural difficulties.

Children's special educational needs are, therefore, very varied. They may range from toilet training to a language development programme, from training in using their eyes, or their hands, or their ears more effectively to encouragement to co-operate and join in with others. In many cases, therefore, what is required is a specially-planned programme tailored to suit the individual. How much evidence is there that children are receiving such individual consideration?

Where there are a number of children with similar types of difficulties, as in a group of children coming from an area where there are many socially disadvantaged homes or a large intake of children for whom English is not the first language, the problem is likely to be easier to deal with than when only one child is affected. Staff realize that adaptations have to be made to the normal programme in order to give opportunities for additional, essential experiences, for example, in language. The smaller the group for whom these special arrangements have to be made, the easier it becomes to overlook them because of the demands of the majority. In the authors' study[6] it was noticeable that individual programmes were devised for children in special schools and units but were seldom drawn up for children with special needs in ordinary schools. Similarly, outside professionals were much more frequently involved in the special sector than in the ordinary groupings. It would seem, therefore, that, while special educational needs may frequently be recognized and dealt with in special units, they are less likely to be tackled in ordinary classrooms, at least as far as young children are concerned. In the non-specialized sector, the children were almost always given the normal programme with only very slight modific- ations when they obviously were in difficulties with it. It can, therefore, be queried whether their developmental differences were being recognized and their special educational needs satisfied.

These special needs are not such as cannot be dealt with by staff who have no additional training, although such train- ing is undoubtedly helpful. Programmes exist to help language development (see Appendix D) and perceptual development[7] and the management of behavioural problems is discussed in a number of books.[8,9] If staff were to work along with a visiting educational psychologist or speech therapist, for example, specific, simple programmes could be drawn up based on identified needs. With parental co-operation, these could be extended into the home so that the child would benefit from a consistent and full-time approach. It will always be difficult to find time to implement these special programmes, but finding the time is part of the responsibility of admitting children with special needs and is no more than their educational right.

ADULT—CHILD INTERACTION

The part played by the adults concerned is crucial in meeting the educational needs of young handicapped children. They should assess these needs, contact other professionals if necessary, work with the parents and plan a treatment pro- gramme. Staff are usually sympathetic towards children with special needs and welcome them into their group providing that the necessary facilities are available and they feel they have enough time and resources to cope. Yet it would seem, as has already been said, that special programmes are seldom devised, unless the child is placed in a specialized unit. The question can, therefore, be raised whether any other special conditions prevail in the ordinary group, for example, do staff talk more to the child with special needs than they do to the others? If they were found to do so, then it could be argued that they were aware of special needs to some extent and were giving extra attention to that child.

Several studies have examined the extent to which adults in nursery and playgroups in general interact with their children.[10,11] These have shown little evidence of sustained conversation, vital in promoting the language development of young children. Instead teachers and leaders more often adopted a supervisory, managerial role and even the imparting of information came well behind the use of language to keep the children organized. Sustained interaction with any one child has also been found to be infrequent.

It would appear that the child with special needs fares little better than his non-handicapped peers. A study of teacher interaction with children in the ordinary school who had a variety of special needs[6] showed that there was little attempt to encourage the quiet, withdrawn child while the demanding restless child was attended to but usually only in an attempt to establish discipline or control. Teachers in the ordinary classrooms appeared to respond to the demands made on them and, if few of these were made, seldom initiated contacts themselves. It has been shown with older children in special schools for severely mentally handicapped children[12] that the interactions were not of this nature. In these classrooms teachers on the whole tried to ignore many of the contacts which the over-demanding children made and to encourage any occasional approach from an inhibited pupil. However, in many cases it would seem to be true to say that children become the focus of adult interaction to the extent that they demand that focus.

Another point which emerged from the study previously mentioned[6] was that teachers did not often praise children but were more prone to reprimand them, a tendency which has also been found in an investigation of older, non-handicapped children.[13] It is especially a pity that this should be so as far as children with special needs are concerned. For them, learning may be difficult and progress slow. It is all the more important that they should receive support from the adults about them and praise for genuine efforts made.

It may seem that an argument is being made for the child with special needs to receive more than a fair share of the staff's time and attention. To some extent it is inevitable that this should be so. At the beginning of the chapter it was pointed out that special needs are additional to normal educational needs. If they are to be satisfied, therefore, special approaches, activities and attention are required and the adults concerned have to accept this. With young children the additional burden need not be excessive. It is part of the philosophy of early education that individual and group concerns should be blended. What is required is that the individually oriented part of the programme should be carefully planned to deal specifically with the needs the child has, and that encouragement should be given to ensure that the child gets as much as possible from the corporate activities. It may be, also, that staff need to reconsider the nature and duration of their interaction with all of their children, including those with special needs.

Where pre-schoolers interact seldom with their age-mates, there would appear to be every reason for helping them to overcome their problems before their isolation becomes established. Typical of these withdrawn children[15] is their tendency to watch others rather than to join in, to be unable to interact constructively even when they do play with others and to avoid imaginative dramatic play. It has been found that these children play better in small, structured groups when either the materials used or the instructions given offer a framework for meaningful interaction. It might also be helpful for an adult to join in play with these children, offering unobtrusive suggestions for elaborating a game or providing a model for more constructive interaction.

Aggressive children, on the other hand, may have to be restrained and encouraged to participate in solitary play or along with one other child for a start. Their aggression may reflect a lack of understanding of how to establish productive contacts with other children or a failure to complete activities, so that they never experience the resultant satisfaction. If adults play with them, without directing their play, they can show how to extend and complete play episodes so that aggressive children can be praised for their efforts, thereby making their previous distractibility or belligerence seem less attractive. A policy of praising behaviour which is incompatible with the aggressive behaviour and which will thereby become favoured at the expense of previous aggressive behaviour makes good sense.

A number of children come into early education from socially disadvantaged backgrounds in which little has been done to encourage skills which would help them to respond to school. For example, their language may be fairly undeveloped, their listening skills poor, their attention span brief and they may be unaccustomed to being with adults for any period of time. Studies have shown[16] that these children also, like the very withdrawn children, seldom indulge in dramatic play where they pretend to be others or engage in imaginary activities. It is a pity that they neglect this aspect of play as it is normally most productive of language; in it children have constantly to explain to each other who they are, what they are doing and how others can interact. Socially disadvantaged children may have to be helped to participate in this type of play by the presence of an understanding adult, who will give guidance but not domination and encourage child—child interaction.

CHILD—CHILD INTERACTION

The development of social skills and contact with age-mates are often the primary considerations in the parents' decision to seek early education for their children. Yet when the events in the nursery experience are looked at closely,[14] it becomes clear that child—child interaction is not always harmonious and constructive. A surprising number of constraints on the child's ability to act or play as he or she wishes appear to exist, some of them stemming from adult organization but many of them arising from contacts with other children. Thus children clash over sharing toys, interrupt each other's games, refuse to co-operate, knock down or knock over other children's constructions and jostle or push, accidentally or deliberately. Children seem to accept this as more or less inevitable and rapidly begin to adopt typical reactions, becoming resigned or belligerent, conciliatory or tearful. Indeed, social maturity includes evolving a style of coping with frustration as well as learning how to share and join in.

Like other children, the handicapped group studied in the authors' survey[6] had their problems in interacting with their peers. Their teachers, in fact, remarked that of the twenty who were looked at in detail, twelve had shown some difficulty in relating to the rest of the class. Of these, five were very aggressive and demanding, some of them to the extent that the others were rather afraid of them. On the other hand, five of the children who had been noted as being very hesitant to approach adults, had no problem in making contact with other children. One significant point about the interaction between the children themselves was shown to be that such contacts were in the main non-verbal. Thus, although some children found it easier to make contact with their peers than with the staff, they were not always deriving as much benefit from the interaction as they might have done had language been involved to regulate and organize the relationships.

The non-handicapped children were sometimes puzzled by the children with special needs, finding it difficult to come to terms with a non-communicating child, for example, or they were curious about a handicap, finding it fascinating to watch a spina bifida child move when out of the wheel-chair. In these young children, there was little evidence of teasing or name-calling. Rather they showed themselves only too eager to help if they could. Aggressive, destructive behaviour was least easy to tolerate and the fairly high number of adult contacts already noted for some children probably reflects this.

FUTURE PLACEMENT

What happens to children with special needs after their experience of early education? To answer this question, the five children who were discussed in the previous chapter can be looked at again. As they are nearly five years of age, decisions have already been taken about their immediate future.

For four of them, in fact, the decision was really taken when they were placed in their pre-school provision. Joyce, Marie, Kathleen and Steven will continue in the schools linked or attached to their present placement. Thus Joyce and Steven will go on in separate special educational establishments, the one in the physically handicapped school and the other in the partially hearing unit. Marie, the other girl with spina bifida, will move into the ordinary reception class and Kathleen's mother expects her to do the same. Only with Roy in the playgroup has a decision to be taken. His reaction to the playgroup has not been very good and it is probable that he will be placed in an ESN(S) school, that is, a special school for severely educationally subnormal children. It had been hoped that his playgroup experience would have enabled him to be moved to an ordinary nursery school, but this has not happened. It is probable that his difficult behaviour, especially his aggression towards other children, proved to be the deciding factor in his case, as intellectually he was at the same level as Kathleen who appears, for the time being at any rate, to be moving on into the ordinary infant school.

How long children with special needs can be educated with their non-handicapped peers is another matter. It seems unlikely that Kathleen, who is severely mentally retarded, will be able to stay long in an ordinary class. Professionals, such as educational psychologists, often adopt a policy of giving a "trial period" in the new provision to see how the child will adapt before decisions are made on the suitability of the placement. Parents should be involved in any such decisions, as well as the staff of the present and proposed school. Perhaps because of a desire to offer such a "trial period", little by way of discussion appeared to have been carried out for the three girls in the five children who have been considered. The placements mentioned are those believed by the mothers and the staff as likely to be offered.

For Marie, also, problems can be foreseen. She manages well in her present class which is on the ground floor. The older infants, however, are on the upper floor and there is no lift or ramp. There will either have to be a re-allocation of rooms or some expensive alterations to the building or Marie will have to be transferred to another school, probably a physically handicapped one like Joyce's, where wheelchairs are not exceptional.

Policy with regard to units for sensory handicaps varies over the country. In the area where Steven is, children remain in a partially hearing unit until they complete their junior schooling and are then transferred to a unit which is fully integrated in a comprehensive school. In other areas, pre-school units are separate from primary age range units and young children may be transferred to the primary unit or to a residential school if the hearing loss is severe; other patterns also exist.

In the study by the present authors[6], mothers expressed considerable worry about their children's educational future.

For those whose children were in special schooling, there was sometimes a feeling of relief that the problem had been recognized and was being coped with. While some remained hopeful that transfer to normal education might take place at some time, they were on the whole realistic and appreciative of the expertise and concern shown by the staff. Parents whose children were in ordinary schooling were happy at this sign of "normalization" but felt that they were not fully enough involved in any discussions which took place with regard to progress. Educational psychologists would be asked by the school to look at a child with special needs, but the parents were not always informed of the results of the assessment. Schools, too, felt that they wanted more say in what happened to these children as they had often invested a great deal of time and effort in the early years of their schooling.

Transfer to another setting and a different regime may be especially upsetting to children with special needs who are just adapting to the pre-school experience. Full records should be sent to the new school so that the child's special needs are recognized and any programme which is being implemented can be continued. Receiving teachers sometimes say they would rather not have reports but keep an open mind about the new children who join their class. While it may benefit the ordinary child not to have his reputation precede him, it would be wrong for information on special needs not to be passed on. Teachers should realize, too, that parents will be tense at a time of change over, until they become accustomed to the new school and their child settles in. Planned visits to the new school can benefit both children and parents and enable new teachers to appreciate the special needs concerned before the move takes place.

Formal schooling with its increased intellectual demands, its quickening of pace and its more structured approach may place demands on children with special needs which they find great difficulty in meeting. Teachers need to show ingenuity and understanding so that they become alert to ways of circumventing the problems facing these children. In this teachers, too, need support from other professionals just as much as the pre-school staff do, and also need to find time to devise and carry out individual programmes. Whatever form of educational provision children with special needs are offered, they are going to require extra consideration from teachers so that their educational experiences may be as helpful to them as possible.

REFERENCES

1. Central Advisory Council for Education (1967), *Children and their Primary Schools*, (The Plowden Report), London: HMSO.

2. HUGHES, M., PINKERTON, G. and PLEWIS, I. (1979), 'Children's difficulties on starting infant school, *Journal of Child Psychology and Psychiatry*, 20, 3, 187—196.

3. PRINGLE, M.L.K. (1975), *The Needs of Children*, London: Hutchinson.

4. ANDERSON, E.M. (1973), *The Disabled School Child*, London: Methuen.

5. TURNER, I.F. (1974), 'Cognitive effects of playgroup attendance', *Irish Journal of Education*, 8, 1, 30—35.

6. CHAZAN, M., LAING, A.F., SHACKLETON BAILEY, M. and JONES, G. (1978), *Some of Our Children*, London: Open Books.

7. TANSLEY, A.E. (1967), *Reading and Remedial Reading*, London: Routledge and Kegan Paul.

8. CARR, J. (1980), *Helping Your Handicapped Child: a step-by-step guide to everyday problems*, Harmondsworth: Penguin.

9. CHAZAN, M., LAING, A.F., JONES, J., HARPER, G.C. and BOLTON, J. (in preparation), *The Management of Behaviour Problems in Young Children: a handbook for teachers*.

10. THOMAS, V. (1973), 'Children's use of language in the nursery', *Educational Research*, 15, 3, 209—216.

11. WOOD, D., McMAHON, L. and CRANSTOUN, Y. (1980), *Working with Underfives*, London: Grant McIntyre.

12. BEVERIDGE, M. and EVANS, P.(1978), 'Classroom interaction: two studies of severely educationally subnormal children', *Research in Education*, 19, 39—48.

13. RUTTER, M. *et al.* (1979), *Fifteen Thousand Hours*, London: Open Books.

14. WOLFSON, B.J. and JACKSON, P.W. (1969), 'An intensive look at the daily experiences of young children', *Research in Education*, 2, 1—12.

15. SCARLETT, W.G. (1980), 'Social isolation from agemates among nursery school children', *J. Ch. Psychol. Psychiat*, 21, 3, 231—240.

16. SMILANSKY, S. (undated), 'An experimental study on the sociodramatic play of culturally disadvantaged pre-school children', Mimeograph.

5

SPEECH AND
LANGUAGE PROBLEMS

Language development is very rapid during the early years, particularly from about 18 months onwards. There is a wide range of individual differences in the time children take to pass through the various stages of speech and language growth, and norms of development can only be approximate. However, by 9 to 12 months, most infants have uttered one or two meaningful words, are able to understand rather more and are beginning to respond to simple commands. Vocabulary then increases at a considerable rate: the 2-year-old is able to use about 250 words, and the 5-year-old has an active vocabulary of over 2,000. Much of the child's speech is comprehensible, even to an outsider, by about 2½ to 3 years, and by 5 he can speak reasonably fluently and correctly, except for a possible confusion of s/f/th. From telescopic utterances of two or three words at about 2, the child gradually increases the length and complexity of the sentences he forms, so that by 5 his sentences are quite involved. By 5, too, the essential rules of grammar have been mastered, and nearly all children are using language for a wide variety of functions — not only to satisfy their personal needs but to interact with others, to reason and plan, and to create their own environment in an imaginative way.[1,2]

The growth of language does not, of course, take place in a vacuum. Although maturation plays its part and the capacity for acquiring language may be at least partly genetically determined,[3] the development of language depends greatly on environmental factors, especially good models of speech and adequate stimulation in the home, preferably supplemented by planned experience in a nursery group from about the age of three. While all members of the family have much to contribute, particularly important is the early every-day contact between child and mother, who is usually closer than anyone else and who helps to determine the emotional climate of the home which affects motivation to learn.

The acquisition of adequate language skills is crucial in the intellectual, emotional and social development of the child. While the role of language in cognitive growth should not be over-stressed, since words can be used without real understanding, it must be recognized that many aspects of thinking are dependent on language, which is the main medium of teaching in schools. Children who lack basic linguistic competence are likely to be educationally disadvantaged from the time they enter school, and to be unable to derive full benefit from their schooling. Ability to communicate is also of importance in emotional and social development. Although social interaction is not entirely dependent on verbal communication, it does not progress very far without language. Young children can make quite a lot of impact with smiles and gestures, but relationships with others are greatly enhanced once they have some language. Children who say little or nothing soon cease to obtain the fullest positive feedback even from their parents, and their social develop-ment is restricted. The acquisition of language helps children to understand their own behaviour and that of others, and therefore to modify their attitudes and actions. An essential condition for maintaining emotional stability is the ability to compare one's thinking and feeling with others; if this is not possible, the child is likely to turn thoughts inwards rather than think in terms of reality.

Since language is so important in the overall development of the child, it follows that any children who are markedly behind their contemporaries in any aspect of linguistic competence during the early years give cause for concern. This chapter discusses the prevalence of speech and language difficulties in under fives, the recognition of such difficulties, and approaches to assessment and treatment.

PREVALENCE OF COMMUNICATION PROBLEMS

Few studies have been carried out on the prevalence of com-munication problems in young children, and it is not possible to give figures that would be widely applicable. It would seem, however, that speech and language difficulties, sufficiently marked to cause concern, are quite common in under fives. In a study carried out as a part of the Newcastle Survey of Child Development,[4] involving 3,300 children, it was found that 133 (4%) failed to use three or more words strung together to make some sort of sense by the age of 36 months. This criterion represents a very marked degree of language retardation, and a considerably higher percentage of under fives can be regarded as having a speech or language problem. In the survey of 7,320 children previously mentioned[5] it was found that 319 children (4.4% of the total sample) had severe problems with speech or language, and a further 518 (7%) mild problems in this area, making 837 in all (11.4%) with one or more problems of some degree. The main types of problem were:

Problem area	Mild problem	Severe problem	Total	% of full sample (7,320)
Speech articulation	455 (6%)	219 (3%)	674	9.2
Expressive language	397 (5%)	159 (2%)	556	7.6
Listening to stories	340 (4%)	126 (2%)	466	6.4
Receptive language	219 (3%)	83 (1%)	302	4.1

Difficulties in speech articulation related to clarity and/or fluency in sound production, ranging from "some lack of clarity and/or fluency" to "speech mostly incomprehensible". Problems of expressive language were recorded in terms of the child's actual use of speech, ranging from "spoken language rather poor for age although he knows the names of most common objects and uses simple sentences" to "very little or no verbal communication". Receptive language referred to children's understanding of what was said to them: difficulties were rated on a range of items, from "understands most of what is said directly to him, but knows fewer words than most children of same age . . ." to "understands no words at all". The section on "Listening to stories" included difficulties ranging from "less interested in stories than most children of age, but will follow a simple story if encouraged" to "has no concept of what a story is — shows no interest". Types of speech and language problems are discussed in the next section.

Among children with physical or mental handicaps, the prevalence of communication difficulties is much higher than in the population at large. Of eighty-two children intensively studied[5] with a variety of handicaps or problems, the majority had speech or language difficulties additional to other disabilities.

TYPES OF PROBLEM

It is not easy to classify speech and language problems in a meaningful way, since there will be a considerable overlap between any categories delineated. However, it may be useful to examine communication difficulties in terms of: those which are experienced in relation to *speech*, particularly immaturity of speech and stammering or stuttering; and those which relate to *language*, seen either as language delay, language impoverishment, or language deviance. In practice, speech and language problems tend to go together, but it is possible for children to have a good understanding of language and to be able to use it well, while their articulation of speech is poor.

The specific speech and language problems of young children with a significant degree of auditory impairment will not be considered in detail in this chapter (see Moores[6] for a discussion of these problems), but will be briefly mentioned here.

The child who is born deaf, or who becomes deaf before the establishment of speech, suffers severe difficulties in acquiring language, however intelligent and advantaged in background. In the past, the main emphasis has been on the development of expressive rather than of inner and receptive language, and on auditory rather than visual language (except for the teaching of lip-reading) in deaf children. The oral approach, however, while logical, has not been very successful, and there is a growing tendency to combine this approach with manual methods (signing or finger-spelling), in the hope that deaf children will be able to communicate with others at an earlier stage and with greater ease than has been possible with oral methods. Whatever approaches are used, it is essential to involve the child and parents in speech and language training as early as possible. Most local authorities provide an effective home-visiting service for children with severe auditory impairment, who may later need placement in a special school or unit, although in some cases integration in the ordinary school may be practicable, with continued specialized help.

It is difficult to generalize about the speech and language difficulties of partially-hearing children, since this category covers a wide range of hearing loss. While in some cases being spoken to clearly and loudly is all that is required, many partially-hearing children will need individual hearing aids. A high proportion of partially-hearing children are able to attend ordinary schools and will make reasonable progress in speech and language, especially when there are no problems additional to the hearing defect and when the degree of loss is fairly slight; others will benefit from attendance at special units, possibly in acoustically treated rooms with loop systems.

Speech

Immaturity of speech

Immaturity of speech is evidenced by faulty articulation of sounds, the most common form of speech or language handicap. The child may omit sounds ("at" for "cat"), substitute one sound for another ("gog" for "dog") or add sounds to words ("sumber" for "summer"). Since all children make these errors in the early stages of language development, and some defects of articulation are still common at 4 or 5, e.g. inability to pronounce sibilants (s, sh, z, ch) or gutturals (g, k), it is difficult to judge when remedial measures are required. However, if articulation is so poor that much of the child's speech is still incomprehensible by the time nursery school age is reached, a professional opinion should be sought then, if not sooner.

Faulty articulation may be related to a variety of factors, in particular (1) physical conditions such as auditory impairment (e.g. high frequency deafness), defects of the tongue, lips or teeth, or cerebral palsy; and (2) intellectual retardation. It may also result from exposure to faulty models of speech at home, such as prolonged baby talk, or indicate regression in the child, perhaps as a reaction to the birth of a sibling towards whom he or she has strong feelings of jealousy. The most effective form of treatment in the case of immature speech is likely to be speech therapy, though additional or alternative measures, for example parent counselling, may be indicated in particular cases.

Stammering/stuttering

Stammering or stuttering refers to a marked hesitancy in speech or an unwarranted repetition of sounds; the term stuttering will be used here to cover both problems. Many young children show a slight stutter at some time during the development of speech, and unless the stuttering is very marked, it is not likely to be considered a cause for concern in under fives. Far more boys than girls are prone to stuttering, which tends to run in families and is often associated with the late acquisition of speech. A variety of theories have been put forward to explain stuttering. Some emphasize causes related to the brain and nervous system, others stress psychological explanations, e.g. the parents may misunderstand the child's normal hesitancies and, through pressure and over-correction, make him highly anxious. No one theory, however, accounts for stuttering in an all-embracing way, and in many cases a combination of causal factors will be found (e.g. constitutional predisposition, emotional conflict and a pressurized environment). No particular form of treatment, either, has been found to be outstandingly successful in cases of stuttering, although a wide range of measures have been tried, including those focusing on the symptom itself (breath-chewing, rate-controlled speech, masking speech by some device) and those of a psychotherapeutic nature (removing sources of conflict, providing a more relaxed environment, modifying reactions to stuttering).[7]

Language

Language delay

Few children will not have begun to use language by the time they are 3 years of age, but a complete absence of speech, coupled with a very restricted understanding of language, may be found in children with profound hearing loss from birth or not long afterwards, who will not be able to acquire speech and language naturally and will need special help beginning as early as possible. There will be some children who begin to talk at a much later stage than is usual, and yet present no other problem and seem to have a normal understanding of language; most of these catch up quite quickly, but they may need help. Degrees of language delay may be caused by a variety of factors, including:

(i) *mental retardation.* It is quite usual for children with a moderate degree of mental retardation not to begin to talk until 21 to 24 months; and for those who are severely retarded not to show evidence of speech until 36 months or even later. Understanding of language is likely to begin rather earlier in both cases; and

(ii) *congenital brain damage.* The development of speech and language is particularly affected in a high proportion of children suffering from cerebral palsy, who often have sensory defects as well as some degree of mental handicap.

Language in young children who have severe visual impairment is not necessarily delayed, but, as language development depends a good deal on visual experience, care needs to be taken to compensate the child for any lack of such experience, for example by associating verbal explanations with the child's handling of objects. In all cases of language delay associated with mental or physical handicap, special measures to promote language growth should be instituted, as a part of an overall plan to help the child's general development.

Language impoverishment

A considerable number of children who are otherwise normal function below the norm and below their own potential in many aspects of language because of inadequate experience and stimulation at home. Such children tend to live in conditions which are generally disadvantageous, though children otherwise advantaged may also suffer from restricted

verbal interaction with adults. Although speech may com-
mence at the usual age, linguistically deprived children may
by 5 years be well behind their contemporaries in both
expressive and receptive language. [8] They would benefit, in
the very early years, from a home-visiting programme which
aims at increasing the mother's involvement, and from a
"compensatory" language programme in a nursery group from
the age of about 3.

Language deviance

Language deviance or disorder is rare compared with other
forms of communication difficulties. In the main, it is seen
as "aphasia" or associated with "autism". The term "aphasia"
is usually applied to children who suffer impairment in the
understanding or expression of language due to brain injury
occurring after language has been acquired; it refers to a
disturbance of the ability to deal with language symbols.
Children may be able to hear and see, but be unable to understand some or all of the language to which they are exposed
("sensory" or "receptive" aphasia); or their vocal apparatus
may be intact, but they will be unable to formulate speech
properly, perhaps not being able to find the right word for
simple objects well within their mental grasp ("motor" or
"expressive" aphasia). Aphasic children usually respond well
to treatment, but will need an extensive period of speech
therapy.

Speech and language disorder, too, is one of the characteristics of children regarded as "autistic", who show a lack
of interest in people and an exceptional resistance to change.
Autistic children may show little or no evidence of speech, or
may have acquired some speech but fail to use it in order to
communicate with others. Those children with some speech
may speak in a sing-song or whisper and have a tendency to
echolalia (repetition of last words or phrase heard), reversal
of pronouns ("you" for "I") and to a confusion of meanings
(e.g. brush/comb). They will need an intensive therapeutic
and educational programme, though progress is likely to be
slow.[9]

DISCOVERY AND ASSESSMENT

Recognizing problems

Parents are not infrequently the first to be concerned about a child's language development. Indeed, until the child joins a nursery group, they may be the only adults in a position to identify speech or language problems, since many under fives say little or nothing when, for example, attending a clinic or even when seen by a health visitor at home. However, although most parents pay a lot of attention to their children's speech from the time it begins, they will usually find it difficult to judge when a problem exists. Further, because of their emotional involvement or a fear of being considered over-anxious, many parents will be reluctant to admit to being worried about their child's development.

This means that responsibility for the identification of communication difficulties rests with nursery staff, since it is important that help should begin as early as possible. As Cooper *et al.*[10] emphasize, it is easier to give such help during the years of rapid development than to try to make up the ground after the age of 5. Outside professionals such as the medical officer, speech therapist or psychologist can be of considerable assistance to nursery staff who would like further investigation of a possible problem, but they will rely greatly on those with first-hand contact with the child in building up a profile of strengths and weaknesses.

Assessing speech and language development

There are two main approaches to the assessment of a child's speech and language development: observation and tests. Young children use language variably in different situations. Some who chatter freely to their mother at home may utter hardly a word in the nursery group, while some who do not say much to adults talk easily to other children. If, therefore, a valid picture of the ways in which the child uses and responds to language is to be obtained, ideally a combination of observation and testing is needed.

It follows, too, that the child should be observed in as

many settings as possible, both, "natural" (e.g. spontaneous play) and "structured" (e.g. specially selected tasks), at home as well as in the nursery group, and in the playground in addition to the classroom. In practice, time and resources rarely permit detailed structured observation, but a number of developmental/observational schedules are available for parents and nursery staff (see Appendix C). These rely mainly on unstructured observation, but provide a rough guide to norms of development, and enable the child's language growth to be seen in a general context.

The completion of an observational schedule will help in the planning of an intervention programme, in particular in deciding upon the starting-point for activities, but the information thus provided will, in many cases, need to be supplemented by tests, preferably given on an individual basis by a psychologist (see Appendix C for a list of tests commonly used with young children). Testing under fives is fraught with difficulties. Most enjoy the one-to-one relationship and the game-like atmosphere engendered, and some respond better in the individual testing situation than in the nursery group. However, it is quite natural for young children to be restless and inattentive when presented with a series of tasks. Consequently, many of them do not do their best on formal tests, particularly on items requiring speech. Test results, therefore, should not be relied on exclusively, especially if they indicate a low level of performance, but should be looked at in the context of all the other information available. Intervention programmes of a specific type (e.g. behaviour modification) may require particular forms of assessment, and these will be discussed in the following section.

INTERVENTION

Although there is still a general shortage of speech therapists, much has been done in recent years to provide support for parents and nursery staff in their efforts to help children who have speech and language difficulties. The varied approaches to such difficulties will be discussed under the following headings:

(1) compensatory strategies in the nursery school
(2) specialist programmes for language delay or deviance
(3) helping mentally handicapped and slow-learning children

Compensatory strategies in the nursery school

During the past two decades, a number of carefully-planned programmes have been developed in the USA to help compensate young children whose language is impoverished as a result of inadequate stimulation at home. In Britain, nursery staff are not greatly attracted to language schemes of a structured or prepackaged nature, and consequently very few specific programmes for disadvantaged children have been devised. Nevertheless, some useful work has been carried out, some of it incorporating ideas gleaned from the American programmes. It will be convenient to consider the different strategies which may be adopted by nursery staff under four headings: traditional (informal) enrichment; planned language stimulation, not using one specific scheme; direct instruction; and instructional dialogue.
(Appendix D gives relevant references and resources.)

Traditional (informal) enrichment

This model sees help and encouragement from adults as providing the best opportunity for children to increase their linguistic skills. The emphasis is on flexibility of approach, free play and self-expression, incidental language learning in an appropriate environment rather than on specific language teaching with highly structured materials or situations, and on unobtrusive guidance rather than direction by the teacher. While informal approaches and child-directed activities are desirable for young children for at least part of the school day, without careful planning there is a danger that children with impoverished language may derive little benefit from nursery school attendance.

Planned language stimulation (not using a prepackaged scheme)

Some nursery groups, while not wishing to be tied to a specific language scheme, want to do more than rely on incidental language learning during the normal activities of the day. They prefer to devote some time, as a team, to the planning of language stimulation and thereby to ensure that each child is definitely involved in language activity. An approach based on the work of Piaget may be adopted, in which understanding through exploration and activity is stressed rather than the use of language for its own sake, the language being linked to the experiences offered.

Direct instruction

This model aims at promoting language development through direct teaching of specific skills. Lessons, usually on a daily basis, are carefully sequenced. The teacher closely follows a detailed manual, and in some cases uses a packaged kit of materials. Drill and repetition tend to be emphasized, although games, stories, puppetry and drama may also play a part in this approach.

Instructional dialogue

This approach focuses on ways of discovering what children can do with language and how nursery staff can stimulate children to use language for a variety of purposes meaningful to them. An important aim is to extend, expand and elaborate the child's language and thinking through interaction with adults. This interaction may be encouraged through regular short individual sessions, or through activities in the nursery group.

Specialist programmes for language delay or deviance

Children with marked language delay or deviance will need a programme of remediation where a specialist is involved.

Some psychologists favour a behaviour modification approach, usually based on the principle of rewarding behaviour to increase the probability that it will recur. Yule and Berger[11] emphasize the importance of the precise description of those aspects of the child's language which are causing anxiety, as well as the detailed analysis of the child's cognitive and general development. They offer no easy solutions to the questions, "Should one teach the child by capitalizing on his strengths or by building up his weaknesses?" and, "Should one attempt to get the child to follow the 'normal' sequence of language development, or should one bypass it?" They suggest tentatively, however, that in cases of delay, normal development might be followed, while with deviant language, radical departures are probably required.

Two other approaches will be outlined briefly here: the work of Jean Cooper and colleagues,[10] and the LARSP programme developed by David Crystal and others.[12]

Helping Language Development, by Jean Cooper, Molly Moodley and Joan Reynell.

This is described as a developmental language programme aimed at helping children aged 2 to 5 with language delay or deviance. It needs to be directed by a professional with a specialist knowledge of early intellectual and language development (e.g. psychologist, speech therapist, medical officer or specialist teacher), but may be carried out by parents or nursery staff. The intervention programme is based on the child's level of functioning in a number of areas: attention control, concept formation, symbolic understanding, verbal comprehension, expressive language, the intellectual use of language (directive-integrative function) and performance abilities (non-linguistic). The aim is to consolidate the present stage of development and help the child to progress to the next developmental stage, while at the same time promoting interaction and balance between the different areas. Guidance is given on planning and carrying out the developmental language programme and on keeping regular records of the child's response and progress.

A Language Assessment, Remediation and Screening Procedure (LARSP) by David Crystal, Paul Fletcher and Michael Garman.

In this scheme, the child's language is sampled through two periods of continuous taping each of fifteen minutes duration. In the first period a record is made of fifteen minutes of conversational interaction in an unstructured, free play situation, using toys rather than pictures or books. The "interviewer" is usually a parent, or therapist if the child knows her well. In the second period, dialogue is encouraged on some aspect of the child's experience which has nothing to do with the immediate play-situation (e.g. family, school or holidays). After a visual record of the taped language has been made and compared with the expected pattern (in terms of age) for normal children, goals for remedial work are set up, and procedures worked out with the therapist. These may involve imitation tasks ("say what I say"), modelled imitation (obtaining spontaneous utterances which follow the therapist's model, e.g. in a highly-structured game situation) and various drill patterns.

Helping mentally handicapped and slow learning children

Young children who are mentally handicapped or who show marked delay in their general development are unlikely to derive much benefit merely from being in a rich language environment, without a well-structured language stimulation programme. Stevens[13] stresses the importance, in the facilitation of language skills in mentally handicapped children, of (i) adults being aware of the ways in which they use words and also non-verbal methods of communication through facial expression and gesture, (ii) creating real-life situations in which language is needed; (iii) an understanding of the various forms and levels of play; (iv) devising a diagnostic prescriptive programme for each individual child based upon direct observation of spontaneous behaviour and regular evaluations of progress; and (v) planned and continuous parent—teacher involvement.

Parents wishing to help a child who is mentally handicapped or slow to talk will find *Let Me Speak* by Jeffree and

McConkey[14] very useful. This book provides practical guidelines for stimulating language, and makes a variety of suggestions for engaging children in language play. Here two other
language schemes recently developed for children with severe
language delay will be outlined: the Schools Council Project
on *The Education of Severely Subnormal Pupils;* and Gillham's
First Words Language Programme.

The Schools Council Education of Severely Educationally Subnormal Pupils Project

The work of this project (which was concerned with a wide
age-range) is described in a book by Leeming and others[15].
This book gives a detailed account of the methods developed
by the Hester Adrian Research Centre at Manchester University, collaborating with the Cheshire Education Authority, to
examine and teach a broad spectrum of language skills. The
methods of assessment used in the project are discussed, and
illustrations given of the teaching strategies adopted. The
research team emphasize the need for teachers to plan
language stimulation with a view to achieving precise and
realistic objectives (e.g. the association of specified objects
with selected parts of the body) rather than broad aims (e.g.
language teaching of body parts); and to make appropriate
demands on children and provide them with feedback on
their responses to those demands. The book includes a
description of *Jim's People*, a curriculum package for mentally
handicapped children which grew out of work carried out at
the Hester Adrian Research Centre. The kit for *Jim's People*,
which is based on an objectives approach, contains ninety-six
picture cards designed to teach specific aspects of language,
both expressive and receptive. All the skills taught are essential
parts of a language curriculum, though the scheme needs to
be supplemented by other approaches.

Gillham's *The First Words Language Programme*[16]

This was designed for use with mentally handicapped children,
but will also be found relevant to other cases of severe
language delay. The programme is based on having to hand

a varied range of easily-acquired stimulus materials, for use in both "formal" (short regular individual teaching sessions) and "informal" teaching (taking advantage of naturally occurring events). A "goal" vocabulary is worked out by selecting words from the developmental lists provided, taking into account the interests of the child and other individual characteristics; language and understanding are stressed, not just speech. Teaching methods include *demonstrating* (focusing the attention of the child on a word and what it refers to), *choosing* (getting the child to show understanding by making a choice, e.g. of one picture from two or three) and *using* (bringing the word into a conversation or improvised story involving, for example, dolls, puppets and models). The programme has the advantage of being relatively simple to put into operation, and also of having a low base-line from which to start.

Non-verbal communication systems

The Schools Council Project on the Education of Severely Educationally Subnormal Pupils, which developed a Communication Behaviour Rating Schedule[15] to assess children at or below the one-word imitation level, found that even the most limited children were able to communicate by a range of behaviours (e.g. pulling, pushing, holding out arms, smiling). Many of the children who make little progress in learning to communicate by verbal means are capable of using systems of non-verbal communication. In the past, there has been some reluctance to resort to such systems in case this should discourage verbal learning, but many teachers now feel that no child should be deprived of the opportunity for developing effective means of communication. Indeed, many children respond to an unexpected degree when increasing demands are made upon them by a non-verbal system, which may serve as a basis and incentive for verbal learning.

A number of different non-verbal systems are now available[17], of which the Paget-Gorman Sign System and Blissmatics are perhaps most often used. The Paget-Gorman System, originally devised for deaf children but now more widely used (especially with the mentally handicapped), has a vocabulary of over 3,000 signs, mostly grouped around a relatively small number of basic signs, following a logical pattern; wherever possible, the signs are descriptive of the concept of the word being signed. Blissmatics, which is used particularly with severely handicapped cerebral-palsied children, is a logical pictograph system of communication, developed from fifty basic shapes, each symbol is easily associated with its meaning. The child is presented with a board with a matrix of symbols on it (ranging from 30 up to 500), arranged by syntactic and semantic category and usually colour-coded. The child communicates by pointing at a sequence of appropriate symbols, and the listening adult uses both ordinary language and the symbol board. Neither the Paget-Gorman nor the Blissmatics system is intended to replace verbal communication.

Both children and involved adults may experience success and satisfaction much more easily when using non-verbal systems than with verbal methods, and children tend to become more aware of their surroundings as they make progress in communication. However, as Leeming *et al.*[15] point out, the existence of a multiplicity of systems means that children moving from one school to another may find themselves being taught by a different method from the one to which they are accustomed. It is essential that a particular system should be taught consistently by the key adults with whom the child comes into contact. The child's day needs to be organized carefully, with the active participation of his family in the encouragement of communication.

CONCLUSION

Speech and language problems in young children are fairly common and stem from a variety of causes, varying from individual to individual. In some cases, they constitute the child's sole or predominant handicap; in others, they are associated with other disabilities — mental, physical or emotional. Whatever the nature and origin of the difficulties, it is important that a careful assessment be carried out and suitable action taken, at an early stage, if possible during the period of very rapid language development between about 18 months and 5 years. All young children need a stimulating environment, including close interaction with adults, if their

language growth is to be facilitated. Those with communication difficulties will require carefully planned attention,
usually involving specialists as well as parents and nursery
staff. In recent years much has been learned about speech
and language problems in under fives, and although there are
still many gaps in our knowledge, this overview has shown
that a good basis exists for sound assessment and well-directed
intervention.

REFERENCES

1. HALLIDAY, M.A.K. (1969), 'Relevant models of language', *Educational Review*, 22, 26–37.

2. TOUGH, J. (1973), *Focus on Meaning: talking to some purpose with young children*, London: Allen and Unwin.

3. LYONS, J. (1970), *Chomsky*, London: Fontana.

4. FUNDUDIS, T., KOLVIN, I. and GARSIDE, R.F. (1980), 'A follow-up of speech retarded children', in HERSOV, L.A. and BERGER, M. (eds.) *Language and Language Disorders in Childhood*, Oxford: Pergamon Press.

5. CHAZAN, M., LAING, A.F., SHACKLETON BAILEY, M. and JONES, G. (1980), *Some of Our Children*, London: Open Books.

6. MOORES, D.F. (1980), *Educating the Deaf: Psychology, Principles and Practices*, London: Houghton Mifflin.

7. IRWIN, A. (1980) *Stammering: Practical Help for All Ages*, Harmondsworth: Penguin.

8. CHAZAN, M., LAING, A.F., COX, T., JACKSON, S. and LLOYD, G. (1976), *Studies of Infant School Children I: Deprivation and School Progress*, Oxford: Blackwell.

9. WING, L. (ed. 1976), *Early Childhood Autism*, 2nd edition, Oxford: Pergamon Press.

10. COOPER, J., MOODLEY, M. and REYNELL, J. (1978), *Helping Language Development*, London: Arnold.

11. YULE, W. and BERGER, M. (1972), 'Behaviour modification principles and speech delay', In RUTTER, M. and MARTIN, J.A.H. (eds.), *The Child with Delayed Speech*, London: Heinemann.

12. CRYSTAL, D., FLETCHER, P. and GARMAN, M. (1976), *A Language Assessment, Remediation and Screening Procedure* (LARSP), London: Arnold.

13. STEVENS, M. (1976), 'Implications of language research for teaching training', in BERRY, P. (1976), *Language and Communication in the Mentally Handicapped*, London: Arnold.

14. JEFFREE, D.M. and McCONKEY, R. (1976), *Let Me Speak*, London: Souvenir Press.

15. LEEMING, K., SWANN, W., COUPE, J. and MITTLER, P. (1979), *Teaching Language and Communication to the Mentally Handicapped* (Schools Council Curriculum Bulletin 8), London: Evans/ Methuen Educational.

16. GILLHAM, W. (1979), *The First Words Language Programme*, London: Allen and Unwin.

17. KIERNAN, C.C., JORDAN, R. and SAUNDERS, C. (1978), *Starting Off*, London: Souvenir Press.

6

BEHAVIOUR PROBLEMS

Between birth and the age of 5, children make considerable progress in their emotional and social development. By about the age of 3, most are ready for group experiences and are able to accept separation from home for a few hours without undue anxiety. As well as enjoying opportunities to be in the company of other children, they are willing to respond to friendly adults whom they meet for the first time. On the whole they are active and happy, reasonably easy to manage both at home and outside. By 5, most are well on the way to gaining some measure of independence and self-control, and show increasing maturity in coping with social situations.

However, the path to amenable, co-operative and consistent behaviour is rarely a smooth one. There will be numerous occasions on which young children will demonstrate frustration at not being able to get their own way. Few under fives do not at times show some insecurity when separated from their parents, or do not resort occasionally to temper tantrums or destructive behaviour. Fear is easily aroused by unexpected events, strangers, loud noises or unfriendly animals. Fatigue or boredom is likely to lead to troublesome conduct, and a severe upset may result in bed-wetting or frightening dreams. In short, almost all young children present some behaviour problems, and tears or anger are never far away even in the case of the happiest child. Under fives should not be expected to maintain adult-like standards of calmness and conformity, or to be co-operative all the time. Indeed, signs that the child is beginning to assert his or her individuality should be welcomed, and it should be recognized that emotional control and social skills are acquired gradually over a lengthy period. It is important, therefore, to try to distinguish between "normal" behaviour and that which suggests a style of response likely to interfere with harmonious development. This is not easy, and a great deal of care must be taken both in identifying children as in need of help and in planning intervention for these children.

This chapter is concerned with the role of parents and nursery staff in the identification, assessment and management of behaviour problems in young children, with some reference to the contribution of the support services and voluntary agencies. It will be of relevance to discuss, first, the nature, prevalence and significance of behaviour problems in under fives.

NATURE AND PREVALENCE OF PROBLEMS

Estimates of the nature and prevalence of behaviour problems in children will vary according to the measures used and the criteria adopted to define what is regarded as a "behaviour problem", as well as the size and composition of the sample. Different people have different degrees of tolerance as far as children's behaviour is concerned, and what is a significant problem to one may be acceptable conduct to another. Children, too, do not act consistently in all situations, and it is commonly found that a child who may be troublesome at home may give no cause for concern in school or playgroup. The findings of particular surveys, therefore, are not necessarily generally applicable. However, recent studies give some indication of the prevalence of behaviour problems in children under 5. Mothers in a London borough were asked about the prevalence of problems in their children (418 in all) at varying stages from 6 weeks to 4½ years.[1] Under 2 years, no severe problems were reported, though 13% of mothers of one-year-olds were worried about their child's behaviour (mainly difficulty in settling to sleep and night waking). The percentage of mothers worried about their child's behaviour was highest at 3 years (23%, falling to 15% at 4½ years); the commonest problems complained of were difficulty in management, attention-seeking and temper tantrums. In another study in London, Richman[2] also found quite a high incidence of behaviour problems shown at home by 3-year-olds: 7% of the sample of 705 children presented a problem rated as moderate or severe, with a further 15% showing mild problems. Differences in the prevalence of problems in boys and girls were not marked, but boys were more prone to overactivity, day and night wetting and soiling, whereas girls were more likely to have fears. In the survey of 7,320 children previously referred to in this book,[3] a two-stage screening procedure showed that 322 children (4.4%) out of the total sample had a severe problem in emotional/behavioural adjustment, and a further 503 (6.9%) a mild problem. Withdrawal, dependence and restlessness were the problems most frequently recorded by health visitors and nursery staff, followed by lack of co-operation with adults, aggressiveness and destructiveness (in order of frequency).

SIGNIFICANCE OF PROBLEMS

As mentioned earlier, emotional and behaviour problems of one kind or another are so common in the early years that it it rarely possible to distinguish between difficulties that are likely to be temporary and those of more lasting significance. Some behaviour problems will disappear quickly, others may continue and even become more serious. Prediction is hazardous, but there is evidence to suggest that children who present *many* or *more extreme* problems of adjustment at the pre-school stage are "at risk" of experiencing later difficulties.[4,5] We do not know precisely what patterns of behaviour are of particular significance in the development of the young child, but it has been found that nursery school children who do not make satisfactory relationships with others, who are withdrawn or very restless, or who show overt separation anxiety and frequent temper tantrums are prone to later adjustment difficulties.[6]

While, therefore, we need to be very hesitant about drawing special attention to any child because he or she has a behaviour problem, there are grounds for taking action in certain cases in order to prevent difficulties from persisting or escalating. Behaviour which interferes with effective functioning or normal social interaction easily becomes fixed, and even if we are unable to predict the consequences of young children's behaviour, it is worth while trying to help children in their current functioning and adjustment. It is also important to try to relieve worry and anxiety in adults who are finding it difficult to cope with behaviour problems.

IDENTIFICATION AND ASSESSMENT

Both parents and nursery staff have an important part to play in the early identification and assessment of emotional and behavioural problems.

Role of parents

Parents have the more difficult role in identifying a child with significant problems, since they are so emotionally involved with their own children that they are less able to take an objective view of their behaviour and to see it in perspective. They are less likely than nursery staff to be in a position to compare the behaviour of their own child with that of others of a similar age, or to form a judgement about the "normality" of behaviour. Even if a child is very difficult to control, the parents may act defensively and deny that there is a problem. Or if they do seek help, they may be told that they are "over-anxious" or that the child "will soon grow out of it". Such rebuffs not only delay help for the child if this is called for, but also cut off the parents from support at a time when it is much needed. Even if parents are being "fussy" or "over-anxious", they should be taken seriously and given the opportunity to talk about their worries, which in many cases will prove to be justified.

Parents may be asked to take on a formal role in the assessment of a child presenting behaviour problems if they are involved in a systematic programme, perhaps under the guidance of a home-visitor or psychologist. They may, for example, be encouraged to observe the child at regular intervals and to keep a record of their observations. This will happen in a minority of cases, but whatever the agency dealing with a problem child, the parents' views will be invaluable in making an assessment of the situation and should always be sought.

Role of nursery staff

The teacher or nursery nurse may well be the first person to identify a child in trouble, and, while it is undesirable that nursery staff should be preoccupied with seeking out problem behaviour, their professional skills can contribute much to the assessment of behavioural difficulties. Careful and thorough observation is a crucial tool in both identification and assessment, and nursery staff often find some kind of schedule or checklist useful in systematizing their observations. A fairly simple, short scale may be all that is required for initial identification: assessment needs to be based on more detailed and precise observation, and should be linked to the response of the child to the various approaches tried out with him. Some nursery staff are satisfied with the description of a child as, say, "aggressive" in the group, but such a description really tells us very little about the child. We need to know - and to relate the information to the strategies used in helping the child — the answers to such questions as "How often is the child aggressive during the group session?" "What, if anything, triggers off aggressive acts; are these initiated by the child, or are they more purposeful in response to specific treatment by others?" "Against whom — or what — is the aggression directed?"[7] Such information, relating as it does to child's behaviour in everyday situations, is of far more value than much of the information which is directly available, say, to a psychologist seeing a child in a clinic.

Most children, even very difficult ones, are surprisingly amenable in the one-to-one situation, and only a very small number of highly disturbed children (e.g. autistic or hyperkinetic) are likely to show evidence of their disturbance irrespective of situation. A comprehensive view of the child will, therefore, include a picture of behaviour in a variety of situations. For examples of screening and assessment instruments useful for nursery staff, see Appendix C.

Whatever schedules or scales are used, care should be taken to build up a picture of the child's strengths as well as weaknesses, and to highlight positive features in development in addition to identifying difficulties and problems.

CAUSATIVE FACTORS

The causation of behaviour problems in the young child is usually very complex, and it is rarely possible to state precisely what has made a child behave in a particular way at any time.

The "precipitating" factor which appears to have been directly responsible for an outburst may be less important than other "predisposing" factors which have helped to bring about an explosive situation. For example, a mild reproof by an adult in school may provoke a violent temper tantrum in a young child, but it may be that the child is reacting to a prolonged experience of stress at home rather than to being told off in the nursery group. Further, it is often difficult to sort out cause and effect, whether, for instance, a speech problem is causing emotional disturbance, or is caused by it. Nor is it always the case that behaviour problems result from extreme or "unusual" stresses and strains, for example when there are changes in the structure of the family (perhaps as a result of illness or bereavement), or when children have to face a new challenge, such as joining a nursery group for the first time.

In spite of the difficulties involved in discovering the factors relating to behaviour difficulties in the young child, it is important to try to ascertain, through careful assessment, what these factors may be in an individual case. This information will be of considerable relevance in deciding what course of action should be taken. In the main, disturbance in young children is likely to be related to material or psychological factors in the home, where the children spend most of their time and where influences have the greatest impact. But it should not be forgotten that children are temperamentally different, and that temperament or emotional disposition seems to be genetically determined to quite an extent. Individuals, even within the same family, vary widely in the way in which they react to stress, and considerable differences in temperament are found in very young children. Some are very placid and rarely cause trouble, others are easily excited and react with intensity even to mild stimulation; some are nearly always happy and cheerful, others are often miserable; and while some are easily discouraged and readily distracted from the activities in which they are engaged, others show much persistence, even in the face of difficulties. The interaction between adult and child is certainly affected by temperamental make-up on both sides: most adults find that they make easier relationships with some children than with others. We now tend to think in terms of interaction — a two-way process — rather than of the child passively responding to his environment. The child helps to shape the environment in many ways — for example, a difficult baby may cause a mother, who was loving to begin with, to reject this child.

The wide range of individual differences among children means that the same approach will not work in every case of a behaviour problem, and the most appropriate strategy for a particular child may be found only after a certain amount of experimentation.

Physical factors

Physical factors, especially handicap or ill-health, may play a part in the causation of behaviour disturbance. Physically handicapped or delicate children will often be frustrated at not being able to do what others are capable of doing, and while most of this frustration is unavoidable, adults can help greatly by ensuring that such children are given tasks at which they can succeed. An association is sometimes found between brain damage and hyperactivity, and although "brain damage" is too readily used as an explanation for behaviour problems, it is desirable that a medical opinion should be sought in cases of extreme restlessness and mobility (as it should be in any case where physical factors are involved and the child is not already under medical supervision).

Delayed general development

Frustration and feelings of inadequacy are also frequently experienced by children who are mentally handicapped or slow in their general development. These children often have difficulty in controlling their impulses and in assessing the demands of the external world, and they take longer than others to achieve some measure of independence. Slow learners are not only more prone to "maladjusted" behaviour reactions than normal children, but such behaviour tends to persist over a much longer period of time. They are also likely to be retarded in speech and language, and as a result their ability to communicate with and relate to others will be impaired, and their self-concepts will not be well formed.

Indeed, delayed language development is bound to have generally adverse effects on the child's emotional and social growth. Often the key to the management of behaviour problems in slow-learning children is to provide them with plenty of well-graded activities, carefully planned to promote their motor, sensory, linguistic and cognitive development and to give them an experience of success.

Factors in the home

Clearly, if the child is not given enough to eat, or if he or she is otherwise neglected or physically abused at home, emotional growth will be affected, but there are many other situations which have a bearing on a child's behaviour, not only within the family circle but outside it. These include the following:

Unsatisfactory housing conditions

In addition to poverty, bad housing conditions can be regarded as a major factor in the break-up of families and the causation of ill-health, strain and disharmony in the home, with con-sequent adverse effects on children's emotional adjustment. The social development of young children will be especially impaired by a lack of space and opportunity for play and other activities both within and outside the home. Living in high-rise, and even low-rise, flats is a particular disadvantage for under fives. Their activities are severely restricted; they are often isolated, with few opportunities to mix with other children; and their mothers tend to suffer from frustration, loneliness and depression. Where there is overcrowding, with children perhaps having to share the same bed, fatigue and irritability in the family circle may well be the result.

A lack of routine at home

Some children are given plenty of warmth and affection at home, but are brought up in an atmosphere of chaos, with little routine or regularity in times of meals or of going to bed. Young children need a coherent framework of routine, if one tempered by occasional flexibility, and those who frequently stay up late at night may be tired, irritable and restless during the day.

Prolonged separation from the mother

If the normal bonds of attachment linking mother and child are broken, perhaps because the mother has to go into hospital or for other reasons, the child may show signs of acute distress, sometimes followed by a period of apathy. In some cases, developmental progress, especially in language and social responsiveness, is slowed down. These effects are not necessarily long lasting, but are likely to be manifest in the child's behaviour outside the home at least for a time. Children suffering a fairly lengthy separation from the mother will need understanding and sensitive handling.

Domestic crises

Even the very young child can be disturbed by open rows or a general atmosphere of tension at home. Parental disharmony has been found to be highly associated with behaviour problems presented by young children at home, and may also result in a child showing considerable anxiety and tension in the nursery group.

Parental illness

Parental ill-health, physical or mental, may contribute to the causation of behaviour problems in young children. It is easy to see how, for example, the relationship between mother and child can be damaged if ill-health prevents the mother from giving the child adequate care, or makes her irritable or moody. Mental illness in the parents, in particular, has been found to be strongly linked with the presence of behaviour problems in pre-school children. As a consequence of mental ill-health, parents may not only be erratic in their handling of the child, but may present a model of anxiety, tension, aggression or even bizarre behaviour which the child will be ready to copy. Not infrequently, a child's behaviour is a reflection of the parents' behaviour.

Unsatisfactory parental attitudes and practices

It is not possible to state with certainty what the association is between parental attitudes and practices and the child's emotional development, and it is important not to make over-simplified interpretations of the relationship between parental behaviour and children's behaviour. However, there is no doubt that most children react sensitively to the way in which they are treated by their parents. Many parents show a wide range of feelings and practices in relation even to a single child rather than settling upon a single pattern, but certain attitudes and practices are highly likely to result in problem behaviour in the child. In particular, three main patterns can be highlighted — rejection, over-protection and inconsistency.

Rejection There are many possible reasons for parental rejection of a child. For instance, the child may be unwanted, as adding to financial difficulties or preventing the pursuit of a career, or because the child is mentally or physically handicapped; the mother may be on her own, without support; the parents may be very young and not ready for the responsibility of bringing up children; or the parents may not understand the child's fundamental need for acceptance and love. Parental rejection, too, takes a variety of forms. In many cases, rejecting parents tend to be unaffectionate, disapproving and hostile to the child, harsh in their methods of control and destructive of the child's confidence and self-image; but in some instances, parents may pamper and indulge a child to conceal their rejection from others and perhaps also from themselves. Or they may vacillate between harshness and indulgence as the mood takes them.

The effects of parental rejection on children are likely to be devastating, although not always immediate. Sooner or later, most children who experience rejection will come to be antagonistic to adults and perhaps also to other children; and they will often be lacking in self-confidence, either withdrawing from challenges or seeking to assert themselves by means of aggression and antisocial behaviour. Rejected children at the nursery group stage will tend to demand a lot of attention and affection which they will often try to obtain by unacceptable means, from nursery staff, who have a difficult task in meeting some of their needs while not being in a position to take over the parental role in these cases.

Over-protection   Over-protective parents prolong infantile care and are reluctant gradually to diminish physical contact with the child. They encourage the child to turn to them immediately for help in the face of any difficulty, however mild. The child is discouraged from becoming less dependent on parental assistance while growing older. Over-protective parents may be permissive and indulgent, satisfying every whim children have and allowing them to do whatever they like; or else they may be dominating, interfering and restrictive. Reasons for over-protective parental attitudes include the child being delicate or handicapped; the parents trying to compensate for affection missing from the marriage or in their own lives; psychological disturbance in the parents, or ignorance of children's needs.

Over-protected children tend to be slow to adapt to new situations, to cling to adults, and to be passive and submissive. They will need considerable time to adjust to school or playgroup, and will benefit from carefully graded social training, which encourages independence and greater participation in activity with others.

Inconsistency   Few parents are entirely consistent in their behaviour towards their children, and indeed a certain amount of flexibility is to be preferred to rigidity in child-rearing practices. However, grossly inconsistent attitudes and behaviour on the part of the parents are likely to be damaging to the child. If the standards set by either parent are fluctuating and unpredictable, or if the parents do not have a reasonably common policy, children will not know where they stand and so will find themselves in an impossible position. They will not be able to learn which of their actions will meet with approval or condemnation, and may as a result develop into indecisive, conflict-ridden individuals. Nursery staff, if they are consistent, can help to provide children with a more coherent framework to their lives, though this will not help the child—parent relationship.

Jealousy and sibling rivalry

By the age of three, the child may have made great strides in learning to relate to and play with brothers or sisters, and will usually get much satisfaction and pleasure from their company. However, it is very common for a certain amount of rivalry to exist among children in the same family, who will vie for their parents' love and attention. Nearly every child, too, under five or six will experience fairly intense feelings of jealousy when a new baby arrives on the scene and demands a lot of parental time. Rivalry and jealousy will be exacerbated when parents have not prepared their child for the new arrival, particularly when this event coincides with entry into the nursery group. Difficulties may also be created when the parents (consciously or unconsciously) give markedly preferential treatment to one of their children.

Factors in the nursery group

Factors relating to the nursery group itself are unlikely to be of major importance in the causation of behaviour problems in young children. Nevertheless, emotional upset in children may result from the way in which they are treated by adults or peers.

Children in nursery groups are, for the most part, handled with great sensitivity by the adults in whose care they are placed, but it is easy to cause some degree of emotional disturbance through carelessly expressed remarks or even covertly-held attitudes relating to children from particular social backgrounds or ethnic groups. To illustrate, a particular girl may be upset by:

(a) an adult's frequent over-reaction to her mis-demeanours, clumsiness or failure to perform a task, especially if the emphasis is put on her own nature — "I've never come across such a terrible child in all my life!" — rather than her actions, thus contributing to her building up of a negative self-image;

(b) adults making a lot of fuss when she wets her-self, causing embarrassment and undue guilt-feelings;

    (c) receiving much less attention from adults than others in the group, which may well happen if she does not demand attention in some way; or

    (d) listening to frightening stories — while most take these in their stride, some children, particularly those from highly disturbed backgrounds, may find them anxiety-provoking.

As the child matures, acceptance by other children in the group becomes increasingly important. Young children are not particularly conscious of individual differences and, in the nursery group, social rejection rarely results from being handicapped or a member of an ethnic minority group. However, some children may be the victims of aggression, or, being somewhat aggressive themselves, have retaliatory action directed at them. It is not always possible to prevent a child from being upset by other children or from becoming socially isolated or rejected, but timely and tactful intervention by an adult may help in potentially explosive situations.

Even without any of the upsetting experiences outlined above, some children find it difficult to accept the initial separation from the mother and may take a long time to adjust to the physical, cognitive and social demands of the nursery group. Putting pressure on these children may exacerbate or prolong their difficulties in adjusting to being with other children.

It is, of course, undesirable to over-protect children within the nursery group or to encourage them to avoid meeting normal challenges. It is also important not to exaggerate the potential sources of upset, but incidents that seem trivial to the adult may cause considerable distress to a child and even result in unwillingness to attend a nursery group.

MANAGEMENT

There is such a wide range of individual differences among children that it is difficult to generalize about the management of behaviour problems. Nevertheless there are certain principles which should be borne in mind by anyone wishing to help a child who is failing to adjust socially or emotionally, and these will be discussed briefly.

Maintaining a positive attitude

It is important to try to maintain a positive attitude towards children who are unresponsive or uncooperative, since the negative or hostile reactions of adults towards such children often create a vicious circle from which there is little chance of escape. If the adults close to the child continue to show that, whatever the provocation and however much the child's actions are disapproved of, they are concerned for and interested in the child, this will help as much as anything to effect an improvement in behaviour. Because of the degree of their emotional attachment to the child, parents find it particularly difficult to remain warm and affectionate when the child challenges their authority in ways that are extremely irritating. It is all too easy, when children are behaving badly, for parents to miss the occasions when they are acting in an acceptable manner, to be provoked themselves into a display of bad temper or to let the child's behaviour control their own. It will help if parents look out for any acceptable behaviour, even if this is minimal to begin with, which they can praise, provide plenty of appropriate materials to occupy the child constructively; and seek opportunities for warm interaction with the child. Adults outside the home usually find it easier than parents to remain calm and positive in dealing with behaviour problems, but even so nursery staff may all too readily label a child as "difficult", "aggressive" or "withdrawn" and come to expect particular modes of behaviour from this child. Too often, the expectations of adults are fulfilled. Stereotyping should be avoided, and a variety of ways of positive interaction with the child sought.

Sharing the problem

Many parents and nursery staff feel that it is a confession of weakness if they admit to being worried by a young child presenting a behaviour problem. They think that they ought to be able to cope on their own, and consequently are reluctant to talk to anyone else about their concern. Such an attitude is only natural, but it sets up barriers to communication with others, and such communication is often essential if intervention is to be timely and appropriate. As children behave so differently in different contexts, it is important that, if the child is attending a nursery group, parents and staff should discuss any problem together in a relaxed, informal way. Not only does the sharing of the problem relieve anxiety, but such a discussion can help a decision to be made about the desirability of seeking assistance from an outside agency. If the child is not attending a nursery group, parents should not be unduly hesitant about asking for advice from the available services (see pages 96—97).

It must be admitted that in discussing a child with a behaviour problem, or by referring the child to an outside agency, the problem can be magnified and receive undue emphasis. Everyone involved should help to avoid this by taking a positive approach, refraining from attaching blame for the problem to particular individuals and ensuring that there is real communication between the various parties concerned.

Having clear aims

It is essential to have clear aims and objectives in planning any kind of intervention, which should be designed to ensure that the child develops the more skilled or more acceptable behaviour that was shown previously. Objectives should be realistic: a very small step in the desired direction can be the beginning of a gradual improvement in behaviour.

INTERVENTION STRATEGIES

A variety of strategies are possible in the management of young children with behaviour problems. The emphasis may need to be on providing guidance, counselling or therapy for the parents rather than on directly changing the child's behaviour. Some parents will be able to accept and benefit from advice on ways of handling the child, others will need to be more closely involved in a systematic programme designed to bring about changes in behaviour, such as a Portage-type scheme or a behaviour modification plan under the guidance of a psychologist. Some parents will be helped by counselling or family therapy to sort out personal problems which may be affecting the child, but a number will be so overwhelmed by their financial difficulties or by the conditions in which they live that practical rather than psychological support must be the first consideration.

If the child is presenting a problem in the nursery group, it will be helpful for staff to work out a programme based on positive and sustained adult—child interaction, both on a one-to-one basis and in group activities. Three approaches, not necessarily mutually exclusive, which may be adopted to bring about behavioural change in the nursery group will be discussed here.

Play activities

Since nursery staff attach a good deal of importance to children's play and are skilful in providing appropriate settings for play activities, it is likely that bringing about changes in behaviour through play will appeal to them more than other, less familiar approaches. It is important that nursery staff should not hesitate to take a leading role, or participate in other ways, in the play of children whose emotional or social development gives cause for concern. This needs to be emphasized, since it has been found that interaction between child and adult in the nursery group is often very limited;[8] left to their own devices, without adult involvement, some children are either unable or unwilling to use their opportunities for play to the best advantage. Through carefully planned play activities (see Appendix E), children presenting varied kinds of problem may be helped to modify their behaviour.

Shy or withdrawn children, for example, will benefit from individual play with an adult before being involved in group activities. Later, they can be encouraged to play alongside others as a prelude to engaging in activities with another child and then in a small group. Aggressive or destructive children will need a much more structured programme of activities than other children, which will keep them constantly occupied and in range of an adult. They should be given plenty of opportunity to let off steam in an acceptable way, but should not be involved in activities that demand too much from the child or that will lead to frustration. Restless and over-active children need to be exposed to as few distractions as possible and to be given carefully graded tasks in which they can achieve early success; some of their activities can take place in a screened-off corner. Demands on concentration can be increased as the weeks go by, every sign of co-operation and attentiveness being praised, however fleeting these may be at first. By the careful selection of materials and games and suitable arrangements of the nursery setting, many situations can be contrived to foster social play among children who find it difficult to relate to or co-operate with others.

Behaviour modification

Some nursery staff will find it difficult, in spite of the many helpful manuals now available (see Appendix E) to develop a behaviour modification programme in any full sense, perhaps because of lack of time, the apparent complexity of the procedures or ethical objections. Even when guided by a psychologist, unless nursery staff are able to follow advice consistently, attempts to implement a behaviour modification programme may well result in confusion.[9] Nevertheless, it is valuable for nursery staff to understand and apply the broad principles of behaviour modification, and to become more positive, consistent and systematic in dealing with behaviour problems. In particular, the application of these principles requires a) thorough observation and assessment; b) setting goals, often based on an analysis of the task involved; c) the modelling and prompting of desired behaviour; and d) rewarding acceptable behaviour immediately and systematically. Behaviour modification techniques are not "manipulative" in a derogatory sense but rather constitute a way of teaching new behaviour that is more systematic than is usually the case and that will help to make the child happier and better adjusted in the long term.

Problem-solving

Problem-solving approaches, pioneered in the USA by Spivack and Shure[10] (see also Appendix E), have much to offer to nursery staff, even if they are not in a position to carry out the comprehensive type of programme developed by those researchers. Essentially, problem-solving approaches aim to help the child to reason and verbalize about aspects of his behaviour rather than resorting to extremes of aggression, destructiveness or withdrawal. As Spivack and Shure emphasize, adults do not always help children to adopt new strategies for resolving their difficulties, if they respond to undesirable behaviour by direct commands, actions or comments on what children "ought" to do: they are thus doing all the thinking for the child. Even explanations as to why particular behaviour reactions are not acceptable are not altogther satisfactory, because if children are emotionally upset they are unlikely to take in such explanations at the time. Instead of suggesting the most acceptable answer to a problem or explaining why particular actions do not meet with approval, it is better for adults to guide and encourage the children themselves to think up their own ideas for resolving the situation to everyone's satisfaction.

The problem-solving approach, then, aims to develop flexible thinking and to show children that there is more than one way of solving a personal problem satisfactorily. In order to develop the language and cognitive skills necessary for successful problem-solving, young children need experience of practising these skills within the security of a small group, and suitable activities can be designed for this purpose (e.g. story-telling, illustrating typical problems; role-playing games, which help children to see another child's point of view; and language activities centred round the concepts needed for problem-solving). The basic principles of the problem-solving approach can be incorporated into normal teaching styles. By guiding children through the "normal" difficulties they meet during the day, nursery staff will help their charges to handle future problems more successfully.

Clearly, "problem-solving" strategies will be more appropriate in the case of brighter and older children in the nursery group, and for those with reasonably well-developed language skills. Nursery staff, too, will have to be careful not to demand excessively high standards of maturity: few of us act on the basis of reason on every occasion, and few of us do not derive some benefit from "letting off steam" at times.

THE ROLE OF THE SUPPORT SERVICES

A number of agencies in Britain offer support to parents and others in dealing with under fives presenting problems of adjustment, although the availability of such help varies from area to area. As a part of the health services, advice may be sought from general practitioners, community physicians, paediatricians or health visitors, any of whom may refer the child to a Child Psychiatric Clinic, usually offering out-patient facilities in a hospital and perhaps also special groups for children and parents.[11] The local education authority also provides help, mainly through its educational psychologists working in a child guidance or school psychological service. Many educational psychologists, in spite of increased pressures from other sources, are endeavouring to see more younger children and to work in nursery groups, collaborating with staff in identification, assessment and intervention.[12] Some arrange workshops for teachers and parents, and work with teachers in setting up behaviour modification programmes. Educational psychologists are also becoming concerned to help parents and schools provide a setting that will help in the prevention of behaviour problems.

As difficulties in the home situation so often lie behind behaviour problems in young children, the social services can play an invaluable part in resolving these difficulties, both through counselling and providing material support where required. Unfortunately, social service departments are often under considerable pressure and may lack the resources to give as much help to families as is needed.

Increasing emphasis is being placed nowadays on voluntary effort, but (apart from the National Society for Autistic Children) there is no specific voluntary organization catering for parents of young children whose predominant problems are emotional or behavioural. However, both the Pre-School Playgroups Association and the Toy Libraries Association are concerned to promote the welfare of young children and their parents in general, including those in difficulty. Organizations, too, such as the National Society for the Prevention of Cruelty to Children (NSPCC) and Save the Children Fund have established playgroups intended to have a therapeutic effect upon the development of pre-school children from disturbed or deprived family backgrounds. There is no doubt that the opportunity for mothers to meet together or just to have a break while their children are actively occupied in a group is of great help all round.

CONCLUSION

This chapter has underlined the importance of taking positive and constructive action, at an early stage, to help young children who present marked behaviour problems, while sounding a cautionary note about the danger of labelling children in any negative way. It has been stressed that, although in some cases it will be necessary to call on an outside agency, both parents and nursery staff have a large part to play in discovering which children are likely to benefit from special attention, as well as in assessing and meeting their needs. The selection of the most suitable approach in any individual case is a difficult and often delicate task, but with sensitivity and flexibility, most children can be helped towards a better adjustment.

REFERENCES

1. JENKINS, S., BAX, M. and HART, H. (1980), 'Behaviour problems in pre-school children', *Journal of Child Psychology and Psychiatry*, 21, 1, 5—18.

2. RICHMAN, N., STEVENSON, J.E. and GRAHAM, P.J. (1975), 'Prevalence of behaviour problems in 3-year-old children: an epidemiological study in a London Borough', *Journal of Child Psychology and Psychiatry*, 16, 4, 277—88.

3. CHAZAN, M., LAING, A.F., SHACKLETON BAILEY, M. and JONES, G.E. (1980), *Some of Our Children: the early education of children with special needs*, London: Open Books.

4. MACFARLANE, J.W., ALLEN, L. and HONZIK, M. (1954), *A Developmental Study of the Behaviour Problems of Normal Children between 21 Months and 14 Years*, California: Univ. of California Press.

5. RICHMAN, N. (1977), 'Short term outcome of behaviour problems in three-year-old children', in GRAHAM, P.J. (ed.) *Epidemiological Approaches in Child Psychiatry*, London: Academic Press.

6. WESTMAN, J.C., RICE, D.L. and BERMANN, E. (1967), 'Nursery school behaviour and later school adjustment', *Amer. J. Orthopsychiat.*, 3, 7, 4, 725—31.

7. LEACH, D.J. and RAYBOULD, E.C. (1977), *Learning and Behaviour Difficulties in School*, London: Open Books.

8. SYLVA, K., ROY, C. and PAINTER, M. (1980), *Childwatching at Playgroup and Nursery School*, London: Grant McIntyre.

9. WARD, J. (1971), 'Modification of deviant classroom behaviour'. *British Journal of Educational Psychology*, 41, 304—13.

10. SPIVACK, G. and SHURE, M.B. (1974), *Social Adjustment of Young Children*, San Francisco: Jossey Bass.

11. BENTOVIM, A. (1973), 'Disturbed and under five', *Special Education*, 62, 2, 31—5.

12. CHAZAN, M. (1979), 'Identification, assessment and treatment: the role of the educational psychologist', In LAING, A.F. (ed.) *Young Children with Special Needs*, Department of Education, University College of Swansea.

7

LOOKING TO THE FUTURE

The preceding chapters have shown that, over the years, considerable changes have taken place in the way in which children with special needs are identified, assessed and educated. In this concluding chapter, the main changes in attitude and practice will be briefly reviewed, with a look towards likely future trends.

WIDENING CONCEPT OF HANDICAP

The concept of handicap has become much broader than in the past, and the preferred term "special needs" is intended to include, in addition to the well-recognized mental and physical handicaps, other conditions which may adversely affect development. Recent studies have found a surprisingly high prevalence of speech and language problems as well as of social and emotional difficulties in young children. Both sets of problems may have serious implications for the child's general development and school progress, as may a combination of relatively mild disabilities. Work on social disadvantage — which has never been an officially recognized category — has shown how much an unstimulating environment can contribute to retardation and learning difficulties.

While the greater awareness of the importance of early identification of special needs is leading to attention being given to a much larger number of young children with developmental difficulties than has hitherto been the case, it is likely that there will gradually be a reduction in the incidence of handicap. Medical knowledge, for example, continues to increase. However, one effect of this has been to keep alive children who previously would not have survived; but raising the borderline between death and life has meant that some children have survived with very serious handicaps. When the hold on life is slight and the damage is extensive and irremediable, the medical profession faces a moral dilemma in deciding how much care should be given to ensure survival, especially when resources are limited. It is to be hoped that, in the future, resources for medical research and early care will be extended and that new discoveries will lead to fewer babies being born with defects or enable handicaps to be more effectively managed than is now the case. To this end, there is a need for better access to genetic counselling for prospective parents. Were this more widely and easily available, the possibility of the birth of a handicapped baby might be lessened, or at least, parental shock at the diagnosis of handicap in their child might be reduced, even if it can never be eliminated.

THINKING IN TERMS OF FUNCTIONAL ABILITIES/ DISABILITIES

There has been an increasing realization that medical categories and even educationally-oriented labels provide very little information about a child's needs, and we are now thinking much more in terms of functional abilities and disabilities, that is in terms of what the child can actually do or not do. A clear and comprehensive profile of the child's assets and problem areas can provide a useful starting point for a developmental and educational programme, whether at home or at school: the child's difficulties should always be seen in the widest possible context, with the emphasis on the positive aspects of his development. Obtaining such a profile means a less constricted view of assessment than has been prevalent in the past. Global measures of intelligence do little to inform one of the child's real strengths and weaknesses and harm may well result from an intelligence quotient being seen out of context. Particularly in the case of young children, developmental scales and checklists have more to offer than traditional intelligence tests. Assessment must, too, be increasingly linked to intervention, rather than stand on its own.

EARLY SUPPORT FOR PARENTS

The importance of effective support for parents being available at the earliest possible stage following initial identification or diagnosis cannot be overemphasized. New approaches are already in evidence. In some areas, district handicap teams, as envisaged by the Court Report,[1] have been set up and in other areas, equivalent bodies have taken on the task of supporting the parents in the early years. One such team approach will be described. In part of a large local authority, a community handicap team has been set up consisting of a doctor, a clinical psychologist, an educational psychologist, a social worker, an occupational therapist, a speech therapist and a physiotherapist. All children with special needs in their "patch" are known to them before school entry, while at school and afterwards. Members of the team visit the homes for which their particular skills seem most relevant and give advice to the parents as well as discussing with them, and in team meetings held once a week, future possibilities. For the young mentally handicapped children, the Portage Scheme[2] is implemented under the direction of the clinical psychologist. If necessary, further expertise from a variety of professions can be called upon. What is provided is continued support, based on careful deliberation, from birth through schooling and on into placement in open employment or sheltered work, where this can be arranged. The strength of the team lies in the continuity of care which it can offer and also in the ease in communication which the weekly meetings make possible. The addition of a headteacher or teacher with special educational expertise would strengthen the team even further.

PARENTAL INVOLVEMENT

Any increase in communication between the various professionals concerned with handicap should prove helpful to parents and is, therefore, to be encouraged. With regard to the parents themselves, the trend is very much in the direction of their greater involvement at every stage of their child's life, especially in the early years. Mother and child interaction at that time lays the foundation of the feelings of competence which the child develops and which influences later adjustment. Early interactions are only too likely to be unsatisfactory when the child has special needs. Turner[3] quotes Spitz as saying, "An infant handicapped by genetic factors, or suffering from paranatal injuries or confusing earliest experiences, is apt to give clues to his needs that are weak, indistinct and contradictory. It would be a difficult task for any mother to satisfy them appropriately" (p 102). It is precisely in this area of difficulty that parents can contribute so much towards diagnosis and assessment as they alone know in fine detail the problems which their child is displaying. Discussion of difficulties with professionals promotes fuller understanding in everyone concerned and should work to the child's benefit.

At the moment, parents are not as effectively involved with their child as they might be. Information on suitable activities to encourage development, suitable routines and even suitable diets is not always available to parents. In some cases, parents do not know about sources of such information, for example, voluntary societies; in others they may not understand fully information which has been given in an over-technical or over-generalized way. Home-visiting schemes and moves to specify a professional who could pass on necessary information in a practical way show what could be done to enable the parents to overcome management difficulties and to provide the best possible environmental conditions for learning and development.

There can be no doubt that the corporate support offered by the playgroup movement to mothers is helpful. Mothers of children without handicaps acknowledge its benefit to them by way of involvement and friendship. For the mothers of children with special needs, there are also benefits in the opportunities for observation and discussion presented and in seeing the adjustment of their child to others. A well-run opportunity group (see Appendix B) can, through careful organization and enthusiasm, raise these children's levels of communication and participation in a quite remarkable way. Even if nursery provision were to be extended for children with special needs, it is beneficial for them to have had early experience of the more informal atmosphere of the playgroup with its highly favourable adult:child ratio.

ENCOURAGING INTEGRATION

We are moving away from the idea that a handicap means education in a physically separate setting and that children with special needs cannot be adequately catered for in the ordinary school. There will, of course, be some children who cannot participate in the life of the ordinary school, or who will benefit from at least temporary placement in a special school or unit. We shall continue to need some special establishments, but these should aim, wherever possible, to transfer their pupils to ordinary classes, and should maintain close contact with mainstream education.

The contribution of playgroups to providing a normal setting for young children with special needs has already been mentioned, and in the future it is likely that more places in nursery schools and classes will be made available to these children. Why is nursery provision seen as being of such importance? In general, nursery education aims to aid the satisfaction of children's needs for curiosity, for recreation, for creativity, for mixing with others, for independence and for competence. In an environment in which they feel secure, and with teachers and aides skilled in responding to their needs with appropriate experiences, children should develop sensitivity to others and responsibility for themselves as well as increasing their intellectual and linguistic abilities. Children with special needs require these opportunities as much as, if not more than, ordinary children. There is a danger, if they are at home most of the time, that they may become overprotected, for sometimes the challenge of copying another child or joining in some activity brings out a response from handicapped children that would not have been expected of them. Even with the improved support which is hoped for, parents may not be able to reproduce such situations in their own home. Children who have intellectual limitations make slow progress and, therefore, should have as prolonged an experience of educational opportunities as possible. For all of these reasons, it is to be hoped that more and more of these children will be offered nursery education.

DEVELOPING EXPERTISE

As has already been said, of course, placement is not enough in itself. Special programmes have to be developed and there are signs that those who can help in this aspect are becoming alerted to this need. The educational sector in particular is realizing more and more that early intervention is not only easier but is also more productive than waiting until children have experienced a number of years of educational inadequacy. As the years pass children learn the habit of not communicating or of not joining in or of grabbing instead of sharing. Deviant behaviour becomes established and soon comes to be expected; this tends to make matters worse as expectations are only too frequently fulfilled. A programme planned specially to circumvent difficulties or to build up weaknesses offers different expectations to the teacher and sets challenges to the child that can be met. Many different professions are moving into the planning of programmes for young children and it is desirable that this should continue.

If teachers in their turn are to respond fully to the changing scene, they need in many cases to develop special skills. With the trend towards increasing integration, teachers in ordinary schools, who in general are in favour of this tendency, need additional training to ensure that children with special needs derive full benefit from being with normal groups. A variety of courses of training, both short term and longer term, should be available, dealing with different kinds of need and at different levels. It would then be possible for teachers to become fully aware of the general principles applicable to working with children with special needs and to acquire specific knowledge about certain handicaps, in particular those with which the teacher has direct contact. Some of this learning could be based on specially-prepared booklets; some could take place through day release to attend seminars on specific problems. Educational psychologists and special advisers could offer guidance in the classroom itself as well as in lectures and workshops. Above all, teachers must not feel isolated and insecure, facing problems which they do not know how to tackle.

Over the past few years programmes aimed at dealing with certain difficulties have become available. At the moment these cover in particular language development (see Chapter 5), perceptual and conceptual development and behavioural management. There will undoubtedly be more work done in these and other areas of development and also in the area of advising teachers how to draw up individualized programmes for specific children. In the United States, for example, many local bodies have issued guidelines to teachers on what is required for the individual planning of programmes and monitoring of progress. There is perhaps a danger of becoming too accountable to parents or others, as the spate of litigation in America shows. But more needs to be done in assessing, planning and monitoring so that the chance element is removed from children's educational experiences. Published programmes can offer useful pointers as to suitable activities or methods and ought to be readily accessible to teachers in their own school libraries.

NEED FOR INCREASED RESOURCES

Some of what is required, for example additional training and resources, will cost money. This is even more the case when the requirements of the support services are taken into account, for not only do teachers require more expertise, so also do family doctors, health visitors, social workers and therapists. Whatever advances are made in scientific knowledge, there will always be a significant proportion of children who will require special consideration, and society should be prepared to devote increasing resources to enabling the needs of these children to be met.

In conclusion, it can be said that changes in attitude may be achieved without vast expenditure. Misunderstanding and ignorance are still common where special needs are concerned. Children are sometimes refused admission to ordinary schools or groups because adults are not prepared to show sufficient tolerance or to exercise their ingenuity; the handicapped may still be shunned or stared at or even feared. One of the main benefits of successful integration is that others come to accept children with special needs as being very like themselves in a great many respects. Perhaps if acceptance of differences were to begin in the early years we could look forward to a society in which having special needs did not mean being set apart in any way.

REFERENCES

1. COMMITTEE ON CHILD HEALTH SERVICES (1976), *Fit for the Future* (The Court Report), London: HMSO.
2. BLUMA, S., SHEARER, M., FROHMAN, A. and HILLIARD, J. (1976), *The Portage Guide to Early Education*, Windsor: NFER.
3. TURNER, J. (1980), *Made for Life*, London: Methuen.

APPENDIX A

SELECTED FURTHER READING AND REFERENCE

BATE, M., JAMES, J. and SMITH, M. (1980 , rev.ed.). *A Review of Tests and Assessments in Early Education*, Windsor: NFER.

CARR, J. (1980), *Helping Your Handicapped Child*, Harmondsworth: Penguin Books.

CHAZAN, M., LAING, A., SHACKLETON BAILEY, M. and JONES, G. (1980), *Some of Our Children*, London: Open Books. (See Appendix C for screening schedules.)

DEPARTMENT OF EDUCATION AND SCIENCE (1978), *Special Educational Needs* (The Warnock Report), London: HMSO.

HUGHES, M. *et al.* (1980), *Nurseries Now*, Harmondsworth: Penguin Books.

JEFFREE, D.M. and McCONKEY, R. (1976), *Let Me Speak*, London: Souvenir Press.

JEFFREE, D.M. McCONKEY, R. and HEWSON, S. (1977), *Let Me Play*, London: Souvenir Press.

PARRY, M. and ARCHER, H. (1974), *Pre-School Education*, London: Macmillan Education.

PRE-SCHOOL PLAYGROUPS ASSOCIATION (1980), *Guidelines for Playgroups with a Handicapped Child*, PPA Publications, Alford House, Aveline Street, London SE11 5DH.

STONE, J. and TAYLOR, F. (1977), *Handbook for Parents with a Handicapped Child*, London: Arrow Books.

APPENDIX B

CARE AND EDUCATION OF YOUNG CHILDREN IN BRITAIN

The provision can, in the main, be grouped under the authority responsible for it, but there are also available private facilities of various kinds (e.g. private nursery schools and childminders).

A. LOCAL EDUCATION AUTHORITY PROVISION

1. *Nursery schools.* These are usually purpose built and take anything from 40 to about 100 children normally for a morning or an afternoon session. Children with special needs are often given priority in admission and it has been estimated that just under 20% of children admitted may have special needs. They are staffed by trained teachers and nursery aides. No fees are charged.

2. *Nursery classes.* These are nursery schools in miniature but are housed in infant or primary schools, wherever a room is available. As with nursery schools, regulations govern the amount of space that must be allowed per child (25 square feet per child) and the number and type of facilities (e.g. wash basins, toilets) which must be available. Nursery classes tend to have a fairly small number of children attending, a factor which has been shown by Bruner (1980) in *Under Five in Britain* (Grant McIntyre) to be helpful in the children's development.

3. *Reception classes.* In a number of authorities, especially in Wales, children are admitted to the reception class of the local infant or primary school before their fifth birthday. They join in with older children and may have a slightly more formal programme than is to be found in the nursery situation. Reception class teachers may have a full-time or a part-time aide (or sometimes no extra help at all) depending on their numbers. As in the case of nursery schools or classes, no fees are charged for attendance.

4. *Special schools and units.* Many special schools (which cater for a variety of special problems e.g. physical and/or mental

handicap, sensory loss, behavioural adjustment) have nursery units attached. Here numbers are small and staffing is fairly generous. Teachers may also have had additional training in the particular area of the handicap. Again, attendance at these units is free of charge.

B.   SOCIAL SERVICES PROVISION

1.   *Day nurseries.*   These provide day-long care for children under the age of 5 years. They are staffed by trained nurses and untrained assistants and charge a small fee, largely to cover the cost of the meals which have to be provided. There is a shortage of this facility in the country and day nurseries often feel themselves to be rather isolated from other provision for young children.

2.   *Playgroups.*   These are voluntary groups under the aegis of Social Services departments, and are organized by a playgroup leader with a number of mothers who are willing to help. Playgroups are normally run on a part-time attendance basis and may not meet every day of the week. A small fee is charged to help defray expenses but some groups do receive small grants to enable them to hire premises or purchase equipment.

3.   *Opportunity groups.*   These are playgroups where about half of those attending are children with special needs. Often other professionals, such as medical social workers, meet the mothers separately while the children are at play under the guidance of mothers of non-handicapped children. As with ordinary playgroups and day nurseries, no fee is charged if parents are unable to meet it.

C.   JOINT VENTURES

In a number of areas, nursery centres are being set up under the joint supervision of the Education and Social Services departments. These offer a nursery school or class facility combined with day care, their hours being such as to help the working mother or the single parent. A small fee is payable. They are staffed by trained teachers and other professionals, assisted by nursery aides.

APPENDIX C

MATERIALS WHICH MIGHT BE USEFUL FOR SCREENING OR ASSESSING YOUNG CHILDREN WITH SPECIAL NEEDS

1. General (see Chapter 1)

Griffiths Mental Development Scale (1954). Intended for use by psychologists or medical personnel. Gives a profile of the child's present level of development in a number of key areas. Discussed in *The Abilities of Babies* (London: University of London Press).

Gunzburg Progress Assessment Chart of Social Development (SEFA Publs., Birmingham). Particularly useful for work with mentally handicapped children.

Let Me Play (1977). A book by D.M. Jeffree, R. McConkey and S. Hewson which not only gives useful suggestions as to how play can be encouraged but also provides charts of different kinds of play so that adults can know where to begin and what to aim for. Obtainable from any bookseller, published by the Souvenir Press.

PIP Developmental Charts (1976). Drawn up by D.M. Jeffree and R. McConkey, these charts cover five areas (physical, social, eye—hand co-ordination, play and language). Useful for children who are slow in developing in one or more of the areas noted. Obtainable from Hodder and Stoughton Educational, Mill Road, Dunton Green, Sevenoaks, Kent.

Portage Check List (1976). Part of the material which comprises the *Portage Guide to Early Education*, devised by S. Bluma, M. Shearer, A. Frohman and J. Hilliard. The kit consists of a box of 580 graded cards plus separate record sheets. Aimed at children with fairly severe learning difficulties. The material is also available in book form, *Parents' Guide to Early Education*. Obtainable from The National Foundation for Educational Research Publishing Co., Darville House, 2 Oxford Road East, Windsor SL4 1DF.

Wood Developmental Tests (1967). Like the Griffiths Scale this is really intended for specialist use. Covers the years from 0—6. Can be obtained by professionals from the Child Development Research Unit, University of Nottingham.

2. Relating to Social and Emotional Adjustment (see Chapter 6)

HERBERT, G.W. (1973), *Social Behaviour Rating Scale.* Occ. Papers of Division of Educational and Child Psychology, British Psychological Society, 4, Autumn 1973, 157—63.

HERBERT, M. (1981), *Behavioural Treatment of Problem Children: a practice manual.* London: Academic Press.

LEACH, D.J. and RAYBOULD, E.C. (1977), *Learning and Behaviour Difficulties in School.* London: Open Books.

RICHMAN, N. and GRAHAM, P.J. (1971), 'A behavioural screening questionnaire for use with 3-year-old children: preliminary findings', *Journal of Child Psychology and Psychiatry.*

SHARP, J.D. and STOTT, D.H. (1976), *Stott-Sharp Effectiveness Motivation Scale Manual,* Windsor: NFER.

THOMPSON, B. (1975), 'Adjustment to school', *Educational Research,* 17, 2, 128—136.

3. Relating to Language Development* (see Chapter 5)

BRIMER, M.A. and DUNN, T.L.M. (1962), *English Picture Vocabulary Test,* (pre-school and Test 1), Windsor; NFER.

GRIFFITHS, R. (1970), *Griffiths Mental Development Scales* (language sub-scale), Taunton: Child Development Research Centre.

HEDRICK, D.L., PRATHER, E.M. and TOBIN, R. (1979), *Sequenced Inventory of Communication Development,* Windsor, NFER.

KIRK, S.A., McCARTHY, J.J., and KIRK, W. (1968), *The Illinois Test of Psychologistic Ability,* Urbana, Illinois: University of Illinois Press.

RENFREW, C.E. (1971), *The Renfrew Language Attainment Scales,* Oxford: Churchill Hospital.

REYNELL, J. (1969), *Reynell Developmental Language Scales,* Windsor: NFER.

SHERIDAN, M.D., *Stycar Language Test,* Windsor: NFER.

WHELDALL, K., MITTLER, P. and HOBSBAUM, A. (1979), *Sentence Comprehension Test* (Experimental Edition) Windsor: NFER.

WOLSKI, W. (1962), *The Michigan Picture Language Inventory,* Ann Arbor: University of Michigan Press.

* Most of these tests are available on a restricted basis only; further information may be obtained from the publishers or distributors.

APPENDIX D

COMPENSATORY STRATEGIES IN THE EARLY YEARS

1. Traditional (Information) Enrichment

PARRY, M. and ARCHER, H. (1974), *Pre-school Education*, London: Macmillan Education.

PARRY, M. and ARCHER, H. (1974), *Two to Five*, London: Macmillan Education (a guide for nursery staff).

2. Planned Language Stimulation (not using one specific scheme)

HARVEY, S. and LEE, T.R. (1974), 'An Experimental Study of Educational Compensation'. In *Educational Priority, Vol. 5: EPA — A Scottish Study*, London: HMSO.

KAMII, C. (1971), 'Evaluation of learning in pre-school education: socio-emotional, perceptual-motor and cognitive development', In BLOOM, B.S., HASTINGS, J.T. and MADAUS, G.F. (eds.), *Handbook on Formative and Summative Evaluation of Student Learning*, New York: McGraw-Hill.

3. Direct Instruction

BEREITER, C.E. and ENGELMANN, S. (1966), *Teaching Disadvantaged Children in the Preschool*, Englewood Cliffs, New Jersey: Prentice-Hall.

DUNN, L.M. and SMITH, L.O. (1964), *Peabody Language Development Kit (Level P)*, Nashville, Tennessee: George Peabody College for Teachers, (see also Quigley and Hudson).

ENGLEMANN, S. and OSBORN, J. (1969), *Distar Language*, Henley-on-Thames: Science Research Associates.

QUIGLEY, H. and HUDSON, M. (1974), *British Manual to the Peabody Language Development Kit (Level P)*. Windsor: NFER.

SHIACH, G.M. (1972), *Teach Them to Speak*, London: Ward Lock Educational.

4. Instructional Dialogue

BLANK, M. (1973), *Teaching Learning in the Preschool: a dialogue approach*, Columbus, Ohio: Charles E. Merrill.

TOUGH, J. (1977), *Talking and Learning*, London: Ward Lock Educational (a set of video-tapes is also available, published by Drake Educational Associates and Ward Lock Educational).

5. Eclectic

DOWNES, G. (1978), *Language Development and the Disadvantaged Child*, Edinburgh: Holmes-McDougall.

GAHAGAN, D.M. and GAHAGAN, G.A. (1970), *Talk Reform*, London: Routledge and Kegan Paul.

APPENDIX E

RESOURCES FOR HELPING YOUNG CHILDREN WITH BEHAVIOUR DIFFICULTIES

1. Play Activities

FREYBURG, J. (1973), 'Increasing imaginative play in urban disadvantaged children through systematic training', in SINGER, J.L. (ed.) *The Child's World of Make Believe: experimental studies of imaginative play*, New York: Academic Press.

JEFFREE, D.M., McCONKEY, R. and HEWSON, S. (1977), *Let Me Play*, London: Souvenir Press.

MANNING, K. and SHARP, A. (1977), *Structuring Play in the Early Years at School*, London: Ward Lock Educational.

SALTZ, E., DIXON, D. and JOHNSON, J. (1977), 'Training disadvantaged preschoolers in various fantasy activities: effects on cognitive functioning and impulse control', *Child Development*, 48, 367—380.

SINGER, D.G. and SINGER, J.L. (1977), *Partners in Play: a step-by-step guide to imaginative play in children*, New York: Harper and Row.

2. Behaviour Modification

AXELROD, S. (1977), *Behaviour Modification for the Classroom Teacher*, New York: McGraw-Hill.

CARR, J. (1980), *Helping Your Handicapped Child*, Harmondsworth: Penguin Books.

O'LEARY, K.D. and O'LEARY, S.G. (1977, 2nd ed.), *Classroom Management: the successful use of behaviour modification*, New York: Pergamon.

PEINE, H.A. and HOWARTH, R. (1975), *Children and Parents*, Harmondsworth: Penguin Books.

WALKER, J.E. and SHEA, T.M. (1976), *Behaviour Modification: a practical approach for educators*, St. Louis: C.V. Mosby.

3. Problem Solving

SHURE, M.B. and SPIVACK, G. (1978), *Problem Solving Techniques in Childrearing*, San Francisco: Jossey-Bass.

SPIVACK, G. and SHURE, M.B. (1974), *Social Adjustment of Young Children: a cognitive approach to solving real-life problems*, San Francisco: Jossey-Bass.

WEISSBERG, R.P. and others (1980), *The Rochester Social Problem Solving Program*, Mimeo. Primary Mental Health Project, Center for Community Study, 575 Mt. Hope Av., Rochester, New York 14620.

AUTHOR INDEX

SUBJECT INDEX